FOOL'S GOLD

AND

OTHER PAPERS

Discovering Genuine Christianity

FRANK P. PARRINO

TATE PUBLISHING & *Enterprises*

This book is lovingly dedicated to my wife Theresa
and to all my fellow workers for the truth.

ACKNOWLEDGEMENTS

I am deeply grateful the following members of the household of the faith that God has brought into my life.

I thank my brother Carlo Pelagri who the Lord used to bring me the good news of salvation in Jesus Christ back in 1975.

To the elders and ministry of Trinity Baptist Church in Montville N. J. where I cut my "spiritual teeth" on the tenets of the Reformed Faith during the early years of my Christian walk.

A word of thanks goes to Pastor Bryan Upton and the many fruitful years at the Bible Fellowship Church on Staten Island N.Y. It was he who gave me the encouragement and opportunity to preach on a monthly basis at our Wednesday evening meetings.

A word of thanks goes to Pastor Scott Stutzman of Kralls Mennonite Church in Lebanon Pennsylvania for his prayers and encouragement.

To Pastor Don Hoaglander of the West Sayville Reformed Bible Church (West Sayville N.Y.). His counsel, prayers, and support are gratefully appreciated. A special word of thanks goes to Pastor Don who graciously agreed to review the manuscript.

A special and heart felt thanks goes to Pastor Paul C. Clarke. He has been my dear brother, spiritual father, and Christian role model for much of my Christian life. I will never forget the years of his love, support, counsel, prayers, and the precious times of fellowship we have shared together. I miss him.

To my wife Theresa I owe a special word of thanks because it was she who kept encouraging me to pursue my writing. Thank you for your love, support, and patience.

Lastly, I am indebted to the rest of my brothers and sisters in Christ not mentioned by name. I thank you all for your love, support, prayers, and fellowship.

CONTENTS

INTRODUCTION

I have spent the last seven years visiting a variety of different churches from the conservative to the liberal. Two years ago I had the opportunity to write several articles for the bi-monthly newsletter of my church. Those articles were first time, very brief (due to limited space), and humble attempts to defend the faith "which was once for all handed down to the saints" (Jude 3) from a practical viewpoint. Those early attempts were a reflection on my "seven year" observations of the worship being conducted, the preaching (or lack thereof), and how Christians interacted with visitors and other church members.

My observations find me concerned for the church of Jesus Christ in this post modern age. The spirit of this age says that there are no absolutes. It successfully sells its philosophy that truth is whatever an individual thinks or wants it to be. The spirit of post modernism offers an almost limitless set of views concerning knowledge, reality, and existence. Truth becomes a piece of clay that can be fashioned into whatever form the person wants it to be. This is a dangerous philosophy. It creates a "free for all" anything goes way of thinking and living. The heeding of these "many voices" will guide one's thinking and behavior that is contrary to the absolute truth of the revealed will of God found in His Word of Truth, the Bible. This is a serious problem that must not go unchecked because it will be found compromising what Christians believe and how they live. Any compromise with the spirit of this age will cause us to be ineffective witnesses for the cause of Christ in society and the world. We who belong to the "household of the faith" need to heed the words of our Lord Jesus Christ who said, "Beware of the false prophets, who come to you in sheep's clothing, but inwardly are ravenous wolves" (Matthew 7:15–16).

I thank God for the many faithful followers of the Lord Jesus Christ I have met and become acquainted with over the course of my Christian life. It is my heart's desire that they continue to grow in the grace and knowledge of our Lord. It is my every day prayer they be bold and effective witnesses for the gospel. However, we must stay on the alert as "soldiers of the cross" concerning what we believe and how we live. There is much that stands under the umbrella of Christianity that is contrary to the teaching of our Lord and His apostles. We must give ear to the timeless message to the seven churches in the book of Revelation. We see conditions there both good and bad that are true of the church of Jesus Christ in every generation.

I have witnessed those who are the faithful followers of the Lord in the midst of the tribulation of this world as the churches at Smyrna and Philadelphia. I have witnessed those who hold the great tenets of the Christian faith in the highest regard. They are also equally zealous for that truth. However, like some in the church at Ephesus they have departed from their first love to God and other Christians (Revelation 2:1–7). There are those who have compromised some of their Christian principles with the spirit of the word-age as in the churches at Pergamum and Thyatira (Revelation 2:12–29). Others are like the church at Sardis. They have a Christian name on the outside but are dead on the inside (Revelation 3:1–6). Then there are those who are lukewarm concerning the things of God like those in the church at Laodicea (Revelation 3:14–22). It is a time to speak. The forces of evil are gathering momentum. Satan knows that his time is short. Our great adversary does his most terrible damage as a deceptive angel of light. It is time to tell the world that as Christians, "Here we stand firm on the sure Word of God." Moreover, it is also a time to act. It is time to put that sure Word into daily practice by living faithful Christian lives according to its precious principles.

Every true Christian desires to walk as Jesus walked. Every true Christian longs to see others come to saving faith in the Lord Jesus Christ. Every true Christian prays for spiritual revival in the church and our nation. In order to prosper spiritually and to be effective witnesses, we must begin to examine ourselves by the light of absolute truth, God's inerrant Word. It is a time for careful spiritual evaluation, a time to examine our ways, a time to confess and forsake our sins, a time to a stand with the Lord and His Anointed, and a time to be fellow workers for the truth in the stations of life God has placed us. It is a time to see the anti-Christian word system for what it really is. It is a time to be consistent faithful followers of our Lord and Savior Jesus Christ in word and deed.

This book reworks several of those earlier attempts at defending our like precious faith in a more thorough, expository, and practical way. It remains an urgent, sincere, and humble attempt to speak the truth in love.

FOOL'S GOLD

An Introduction to the First Letter of John

✠

"Fool's gold, yep, that's what you found friend, fool's gold." "How do you know?" replied the anxious sandy haired prospector. "I've been panning the river three miles north of here for ten months. How do you know this isn't the real thing?" With one eye on the prospector and the other on the prized precious stones lying unwrapped before him in a dirty red handkerchief, the calm confident old man responded in a loud voice, "I've seen this stuff hundreds of times. I'm telling you it's not gold." Before the tall stocky build "gold digger" could say another word, the old timer quickly grabbed a nearby blackened heavy cast iron pot, placed it on a large flat rounded stone lying on the cluttered counter, squirted some lighter fluid from a dented rusty can, and tossed in the "find" along with a lighted match. The wide eyed young man put his hands over his head as he watched in startled silence. Quickly a foot high flame arose. In a few minutes the small exchange house was shrouded in a cloud of yellowish white smoke accompanied by such a bad odor that both men hurried out the back door for a breath of fresh air. The gray bearded old man, looking down the barrel of his steady pointed finger, said to the confused prospector, "My friend, this is what determines real gold from fool's gold. Genuine gold does not smoke and reek like what we just witnessed."

Today many people claim to be Christians. America is considered a Christian nation. A series of Gallup polls conduced during the first six months of 2005 revealed the following statistics: 56% said that religion was important in their lives. Another 26% said it was fairly important in their lives. Eight out of ten identified with some form of the Christian religion. Four out of ten said they attended church on a regular basis. Surveys are not perfect but they do reflect as in this case to a fairly accurate degree the spiritual climate of the day. I find such statistics disturbing. These numbers suggest that many are not in reality what they claim to be, Christians, believers in and followers of the Lord Jesus Christ. In the Book of Revelation, the church (the body of Christ) is symbolized by "seven golden lamp stands" (Rev. 1:12). Golden means that in God's eyes His church is valuable, precious, and pure. No base or impure metal belongs in her. As a lamp stand the church in her witness to others is to hold up the light of the gospel in this sin dark world. However, as a line from an old country song says, "all that glitters is not gold." There is a good amount of "fool's gold" afoot in the rivers of Christianity. There is much that smokes and reeks when tested by the fire of God's Word of Truth.

A dear friend of mine who has gone to be with the Lord, some years ago related the following story to me. There were two young women who made a profession of faith in Jesus Christ. They enthusiastically told friends, neighbors, and relatives they were born again Christians. They attended church on a regular basis. One sister was eighteen-years-old. The other was twenty. Both were living at home with their mom. Mrs. B was open minded and interested in what her daughters had to say about Jesus. A year had passed but the mother had not yet trusted Christ as her Savior and Lord. One summer evening while talking around the dinner table, the older sibling quickly jumped up. In a frustrated tone of voice she blurted out, "Ma! When you get saved there is a change in you." The mother swiftly shot back in a firm but calm voice, "Change? What change? I see no change in you or your sister."

It takes more than believing facts about Christianity, knowing all its words and names, identifying with it, and going to church to be a true Christian. No doubt you have heard the expression, "actions speak louder than words." What you believe will demonstrate itself in how you conduct your life. A few months after those words were exchanged, the younger sister like Demas, "having loved this present world," deserted the faith she once professed (see 2 Timothy 4:10). The older sister followed speedily on her sister's heels as she became indifferent to the things of God. There was no change as their mom sadly but accurately observed. Why? They simply were not born from above. Not in Christ. Not united to Him by saving faith. They did not exercise "repentance toward God and faith in our Lord Jesus Christ" (Acts 20:21). There was no evidence of what Paul calls a "new creature; the old things passed away; behold, new things have come" (2 Corinthians 5:17). Billy Graham put it most directly when he said in one of his last sermons in New York, "We are all sinners and in need of *radical transformation*." When we observe what is believed and the lifestyles followed by not a few of professing Christians we find something very different from "the faith which was once for all handed down to the saints" (Jude 3). Saints are not simply some elite spiritual group of a particular church denomination who get a spot allotted to them on the church calendar. No. Saints literally mean *holy ones*. Saints are what God's Word the Bible calls all the true followers of the Lord Jesus Christ. Such are united to Christ. This being so, saints have a new view of Christ. The Lord Jesus is now most precious to them. Saints have a new purpose for living. They now live not to please themselves but God who is their mighty Savior from sin and Lord of their life. Saints have a new focal point of concern. Heavenly and eternal things are first and foremost on their minds and in their hearts. They have experienced radically transformed lives not simply a moral transformation where they may give up a particular vice that has plagued them in life. Saints walk (conduct themselves) in the same manner as Jesus walked (1 John 2:6). The reformer Martin Luther wrote, "God does not want hearers and repeaters of words, but doers and followers who exercise themselves in the faith that worketh by love."[1] Saints are those who have been washed from their sins, justified, and sanctified or set apart unto God for holiness. To be justified means to be set right before God on the basis of Christ's atoning death. These are the genuine gold nuggets found in the rivers of Christianity.

A Christian friend recently asked me, "How could some people claim to be Christians while deliberately hurting others to get ahead in the work place?" "How can Christians be leading participants in stinging office gossip?" "Why do churches have cliques, a select inner circle so to speak, who give visitors and even other church members the feeling they don't belong?" Such questions are not to be taken lightly. As those who claim the title of Christian do we have a genuine concern for other believers? How about unsaved friends, relatives, neighbors, and co workers? Are we concerned about their temporal and spiritual well being? Are we doers of God's Word? Do others stand up and take notice of us? Do they see something different about us? Do they take us aside and ask, "What makes you say and act differently from everyone else?" Or do we just blend in, go with the flow, and conduct ourselves as everyone else thus marring our witness for the Lord? Concerning those who lay claim to the fair name of Christ, someone once said, "None should wear the name of saints but those who have the nature of saints [. . .] worthy of condemnation are those who profess to be saints, but have nothing saintly about their character and life."[2] What was in the head and on the lips of the two young women in our real life story was not found in their heart. The heart is the well from which springs all the issues of life. It was not changed and radically renewed by the grace of God. Certainly there is something unpleasant that smokes and reeks in the atmosphere of Christendom.

Since the beginning the church of Jesus Christ has been engaged in a continual battle to maintain the purity of her faith and practice against those who endlessly labor to pervert the gospel. These attacks in the form of persecution and error have come from both without and within the church. Satan, the father of lies, the arch enemy of Christ and His people, has done his most destructive work by assaulting the church through deception. The old paths of gospel truth are under constant siege. Gospel truths are criticized, ignored, discarded, or redefined to be more up to date, accommodating, and non offensive to all groups. The one way of salvation through Jesus Christ alone has many paths appended to it. Absolute truth is scorned upon. It is either tossed out the window as irrelevant or put on a shelf where it just gathers dust in the attic of this world. The God drawn straight lines of absolute truth have been bent, blurred, broken, or erased so that we find many doing what is right in their own eyes. Sin is tolerated, made excuses for, and increasingly accepted as normal behavior. The Lord's Day is used by many as any other day of the week. Just look at how sports have become the "golden calf" on any given Sunday. There are far more people, sadly Christian people, found in the shopping malls than in the Lord's house. How many Christians truly consider the Sabbath a delight? Is that special day a delight that expresses itself in the worship of God and other appropriate spiritual exercises? Worldliness has made great inroads into the lives of professing Christians. Its ways, opinions, approvals, pleasures, and attitudes have permeated not a few thoughts, words, and deeds. As a result hypocrisy has stained the witness of many who stand under the banner of Christianity. Sound doctrine, separation from the world, and holiness of life which are the characteristics of genuine Christians are becoming rarer with each passing year. When I was a teenager, I remember a songwriter asking the question, "How can I be sure in a world that is constantly changing?" How can we be sure in this same world that is constantly changing as to what is genuine Christianity amidst all the "authoritative" voices which stake a claim to the truth? How can we be sure what is historic and genuine Christianity when the absolutes of what we believe and how we live as Christians are being washed away by the watchword of the day, "get with the times people." How can we distinguish the true Biblical Christian from the one who merely professes to be one? This is where the first letter of John helps us to determine what genuine Christianity is. We shall briefly consider some of its leading points to help us answer our question.

First John can be described as a late, a general, and a crisis letter. The beloved apostle is writing near the end of the first century. Most conservative scholars place the date of his writing about the year 85. It is an unusual letter in that it lacks the typical format of a letter. First John is not addressed to any specific person or church as the other New Testament letters. We also find no name or signature of the writer. It is a general letter full of a pastoral content directed not to a particular church but to a wide circle of churches most likely located in Asia Minor (modern day Turkey). This area is where it is believed John resided in the later years of his life. It is a crisis letter because Satan and his minions were at their wicked work seeking to distort and corrupt the faith (doctrine) and practice (manner of living) of the church of Jesus Christ. The immediate problem faced by Christians at the time of John's writing was a group of false teachers who threatened the fellowship of the churches. Questioning the absolute truths of Christianity as taught by our Lord and His apostles, the false teachers stood on their soap boxes proclaiming a new way of thinking and a new way of living that didn't square with the gospel. The movement which spawned these false views was a form of proto-Gnosticism. Although Gnosticism did not come into full bloom till later in the second century, it was beginning to take root and sprout its errors in the fields of Christianity during the days of the apostles. This movement takes its name from the Greek word for knowledge which is gnosis. These self proclaimed knowing ones offered a secret gnosis which was the way of salvation but only for those initiated into the "mysteries" of their system. Note that Gnosticism developed in the incubator of Jewish, Persian, Syrian, Egyptian, and Greek religion, philosophy, and culture. This melting pot of "faith and practice" took on just enough Christianity to make it a formidable foe of the Faith. In the days of the apostles we see Gnosticism taking shape in the form of a false dualism. The Gnostics believed in two principles or gods. One was good and the other evil. What concerns us here is that this dualism led to speculations concerning angels and spirits. This in turn led to false views of Christ. The other tenet was a false view concerning the living of the Christian life. To these two errors we now turn.

What was this new thinking or system of belief that came knocking at the door of the churches? The false teachers taught that matter (e.g. the human body) was evil but the spirit good. Since the physical body was evil it was impossible for Christ to have a real physical body. He was thought to be a phantom, an apparition, and only apparently real. This view came to be known as Docetism which derived its name from the Greek word *to seem*. The result was the denial of the real incarnation of Jesus Christ. The incarnation is one of the foundational truths of historic Christianity. It means that the eternal Son of God became human, was born of the Virgin Mary, and without sin. He took the human nature without in any way or degree lessening His Divine nature. The gospel records are clear that Jesus Christ had a real physical tangible body. His resurrection too was a bodily one (Matthew 28:9; Luke 24:38–43; John 20:17; 25–29; John 21; Acts 1:3–4). Although this is not the main error John was addressing, he demolishes any such notion by stating in the prolog of the letter that the apostles were "eye, ear, and touch" witnesses of the Lord Jesus before and after His glorious resurrection from the dead (1 John 1:1–4). "We saw (a word meaning scrutinized carefully and thoughtfully) His glory." (John 1:14). Moreover this dualism, that there are two opposite gods, resulted in the good god being approached only through a series of intermediaries or middle beings. This brings us to the prime error that the apostle is refuting. This error was perpetrated by one named Cerinthus who was a contemporary of John. Clinging to the idea that matter was evil and the spirit good, Cerinthus made a distinction between the man Jesus and the Divine Christ. Jesus was born by normal human conception. Joseph was his true biological father. Jesus was more distinguished in character and life than ordinary men but nonetheless was only a man. The heavenly Christ was the divine messenger or chief middle being. He descended upon the man Jesus at his baptism but departed from him prior to his passion and death upon the cross. It was the man Jesus who suffered and died. Here again we have a denial of the real incarnation of the Lord Jesus Christ as touching His virgin birth and Deity. Cerinthus and his followers divided the two natures of Christ. They failed to grasp that the Divine and human natures of Christ are in the one Person forever without any mixture or confusion. The apostle calls attention to the fact that all who deny the real incarnation of Jesus Christ are nothing but deceivers, antichrists, and without a Savior (1 John 2:22–23; 4:1–3; 2 John 7).

What was the new morality that was knocking at the door of

the churches? It concerned itself with the nature of the Christian life. The dualism touching matter and spirit led the false teachers down the road of two dangerous extremes. One was asceticism which is the practice of rigid self denial in order to win divine favor. The other was licentiousness which is the lack of moral restraint. We meet the former extreme mentioned by Paul in Colossians 2:20–23 and 1 Timothy 4:1–3. However, it is this other extreme, licentiousness that is thrust into the spotlight by John. To the minds of the heralds of the new morality, the body was evil and doomed to expire. On the other hand, since the spirit was independent of the body it was not subject to evil. It did not matter at all what you did. The spirit was unaffected by how you conducted yourself and remained undefiled. Bottom line: it gave a person license to sin. Live for the moment. Eat, drink, and be merry. Get all the gusto you can out of life. They placed themselves above the moral law of God. Being typical of all sinners they asserted themselves against the revealed will of God while serving their own selfish appetites. Nothing was sinful to them. Just as the error of the new theology left them without a genuine Savior so did the error of the new morality. It had the added misery of leaving them in the utter chaos of rebellion against God. It blinded them to the warning of Scripture that without sanctification (holiness of life) no one will see the Lord (see Hebrews 12:14). This practical error is referred to by the apostle in such places as 1 John 1:8, 10, 2:4, and 3:4–10.

To compound the problem these false teachers arose from the very ranks of the church. They were at one time active members of the fellowship. Their views were so divergent from the apostolic teaching about the person and work of Christ and the living of the Christian life, they left the fellowship (1 John 2:19). They didn't leave empty handed. The new teachers took some of the members with them. This caused quit a stir. One of the most troubling things that can occur in a church is when the fundamental truths of the gospel are challenged by a new set of ideas or a redressing of old ones found in the wrappings of Christian doctrine. Such erroneous views can cause confusion, divisions, bad feelings, discord, and even hostility amongst the membership if they are allowed to gain a foot hold. In the churches of Asia Minor, the false teachers and their converts left the fellowship which raised questions and unsettled the faith of the churches. John writes his pastoral letter to expose the false teachers, their erroneous views, and to reassure those who remained in the fellowship of the gospel truths they were taught, embraced, and endeavored to live by. To do this John sets up three tests that distinguish genuine Christians from those who profess to be so.

The tests involve one that is Christological and two that are ethical. The first is the doctrinal or test of truth. What does a person believe about Jesus Christ? Secondly, there is the social or test of love. Does the person love God and others? Thirdly, there is the moral or test of righteousness. Does the person obey God's commandments? We begin by stating that these three tests are arranged in a series of three cycles. The first cycle is found in 1 John 1:5–2:28. The apostle addresses the Christian life in terms of an intimate fellowship between God, His people, and one another. Those who belong to this unique fellowship are marked by adhering to the truth (doctrinal test), love (social test) and righteousness (moral test). Concerning this fellowship, we must note that it is a key concept. John establishes its importance right from the start (1 John 1:3, 6–7). Fellowship is translated as such by the Greek word *koinonia*. It basically means to share something in common with others or a joint participation in a common interest. Christians share a common faith, a common relationship to God, and to one another. The followers of Christ participate together in a common goal for the cause of Christ. Those who belong to this special fellowship have correct (Biblical) views of the Person and work of Christ along with His teachings. The very fabric of this unique fellowship is thus interwoven with truth, love, and righteousness. These are the spiritual brand marks found on the genuine Christian.

The second cycle is contained in 1 John 2:18–4:1–6. Here we are presented with the Christian life as a Divine son ship. Only those born of God are the true children of God. Only those who have been born from above constitute the true family of God. Being in right relationship with God they again are marked by sticking to the truth as it is in Jesus. They are characterized by love for God and others. The child of the living God is distinguished by righteousness which manifests itself in a path of obedience to the Lord and His commandments. The last cycle is found in 1 John 4:7–5:20. Here we find the three tests woven together. We are presented with truth (faith), love, and righteousness (obedience) from different angles which bring in its wake blessed assurance to true believers in their Christian walk and relationship to God.

As the apostle Paul neared the end of his life and ministry he wrote to young pastor Timothy, "Oh Timothy, guard what has been entrusted to you, avoiding empty and worldly chatter and the opposing arguments of what is falsely called 'Knowledge' which some have professed and thus gone astray from the faith" (1 Timothy 6:20–21). Nothing could be more descriptive of John's proto-Gnostic opponents. He singles them out in the letter as those who deserted the fellowship, walk in darkness, liars, deceivers, antichrists, loveless toward others, haters of God and His children, lovers of the world, those who practice lawlessness (sin), and those enslaved by the evil one. John was very fond of making contrasts in his letter (e.g. truth vs. error, light vs. darkness). He also had a great deal to say about knowledge. The apostle continually contrasted the true knowledge of the gospel over against the false knowledge of the new thinkers. The proto-Gnostic brand of knowledge was of the intellectual and mystical sort. The possessors of such knowledge only made them arrogant, loveless, and prejudiced against anyone who didn't agree with their views. What was falsely called knowledge was devoid of appropriate actions. Again we emphasize that truth, love, and righteousness are essential elements of the true Christian's spiritual fiber. They are the environment surrounding genuine Christian fellowship with our Triune God and one another. This fellowship is based on the very nature of God Himself who is pure Light and perfect love. The knowledge that John imparts is rooted in Jesus Christ who alone is the way, the truth, and the life (John 14:6). In Christ alone are hidden all the treasures of wisdom and knowledge (Colossians 2:3). Such glorious treasures are revealed to us by God in His Word and by His Spirit. This knowledge is not merely of the intellectual kind. It is a sanctified knowledge that enters the mind but doesn't stop at that level. Once it takes hold of us as the Spirit of God works in us, this knowledge sinks down deep into our hearts, stirring the emotions, and proving itself by our actions. The apostle then in expounding the test of love, shows that we don't love with only words but by actions (deeds) and truth (1 John 3:16–20). The test of righteousness is simply but profoundly this: do we keep the commandments of God? Do we "walk the talk" as the saying goes? Jesus declares, "If you love Me you will keep My commandments" (John 14:15). The genuine Christian doesn't pick and choose what commandments he or she will obey. Love is our response to what God has done for us in rescuing us from our sins and restoring us to fellowship with Himself. Our lives become marked by obedience to the Lord. We delight to do God's will. This knowledge is intimate and personal. It is to know "the only true God and Jesus Christ whom You have sent" (John 17:3). It is the "knowledge of the truth which is according to godliness" (Titus 1:1). As he builds upon the three tests John is hammering in the fasteners of this real knowledge. He says for example, "By this we know that we have come to know Him, if we keep His commandments." "We know we have passed out of death into life, because we love the brethren" (1 John 2:3; 3:14). "By this we know the spirit of truth and the spirit of error" (1 John 4:6). Here the apostle provides the Biblical criteria concerning the incarnation of Jesus Christ. All these fasteners of real knowledge are intended to discover our true standing with God, anchor our faith, and provide us with the assurance we need to live before God in total trust and calm confidence. To know the truth is the master key to getting everything else right especially in matters of faith (belief) and practice.

We have briefly gleaned through the first letter of John to see how the apostle distinguishes the "fool's gold" brand of Christianity from that of the genuine "gold nuggets." My friends, the teachings of the proto-Gnostics are not simply errors that circulated in the first century and went away. These false teachings have resurfaced and reshaped themselves over and over again with the rise of each new generation. Sadly they are very much alive and kicking today. False teaching comes to us wearing a new set of clothing. One simply needs to read a little church history to see that this is true. Let us briefly look at a few examples. Touching the doctrinal or test of truth (the Christological test) there was the great Arian controversy of the fourth century. This battle for the truth centered on the critical question: Who is Jesus Christ? Arius, a presbyter from the Alexandrian church, came on the scene denying the deity of Jesus Christ. He taught that before the incarnation, the Logos or Word (Son) was the first and highest of created beings. There was a time when the Son did not exist. At a point in time the Son was created out of nothing by God. Only the Father was true God. Arius was a popular teacher who nearly succeeded in winning the majority of the church to his incorrect view. Today we have the Jehovah's Witnesses. They have a view about Christ very similar to that of Arius. Well organized and well schooled they have successfully dug their claws of deception into the minds of many poor deluded souls. Do we not hear echoes of John's words, "Whoever denies the Son [as to His true person] does not have the Father" (I John 2:23)?

As for the ethical tests (love and righteousness) I call your attention to the Anabaptist wing of the sixteenth century reformation in Europe. For several hundred years the Anabaptists have been unjustly cast in a bad light. Most people are only acquainted with an extreme fringe group or individual that gets all the press in the history books. The vast majority of Anabaptists (which means re-baptizers) stressed following Jesus and holiness of life. If you read some of the more numerous and objective material now available you will discover that these believers were people who truly loved the Lord. Their lives were characterized by remarkable piety and modesty. One of the early Anabaptists was a converted Benedictine monk, Michael Sattler. This godly man, who gave his life for the cause of Christ, is associated with one of the early Anabaptist confessions of faith known as the Schleitheim Articles (1527). In its introductory remarks we read,

A very great offense has been introduced by some false brothers among us, whereby several have turned away from the faith, *thinking to practice and observe* the freedom of the Spirit and of Christ. But such have fallen short of the truth and (to their own consternation) are given over to *lasciviousness and license of the flesh.* They have esteemed that faith and love *may do and permit everything* and that *nothing can harm them*, since they are "believers"[3] (italics mine).

I put those specific words in italics to underscore the point that even in the sixteenth century this is just what the false professors of the faith were doing as in John's day. Listen to the echoes of John's words, "If we say we have fellowship with Him and yet walk in the darkness, we lie and do not practice the truth." "If we say that we have no sin, we are deceiving ourselves and the truth is not in us." "If we say that we have not sinned, we make Him a liar and His word is not in us" "No one who is born of God practices sin." "[. . .] for the one who does not love his brother, whom he has seen, cannot love God whom he has not seen" (1 John 1:6, 8, 10; 4:20).

Lastly consider the late nineteenth century Downgrade Controversy in which the reformed Baptist pastor and preacher, Charles Spurgeon fought his last battle for the truth of the gospel. The nineteenth century was not only known as the "age of reason" it was the time when the tide of "human reason" washed ashore on the banks of Christianity. Like a deadly parasite, human reason invaded the body of Christian theology. Beginning with the rejection of the inspiration, infallibility, and authority of the Bible, it wasn't long before every denomination was infected by grave errors in the matters of faith and practice. Even Christian seminaries and colleges succumbed to the errors of the "new" thinkers. Every truth of historic Christianity was attacked by them. The person and work of Christ was either rejected or compromised. Hell was let loose and vanquished. The imputation of sin was called a myth. Christ's bodily resurrection was rejected, spiritualized, or considered the result of His follower's hysteria. Space fails me to mention many more errors. Everything went sliding downhill into a giant ball of error called Modernism. Let me mention that it has been about 114 years since the passing of Spurgeon. The error of Modernism that Spurgeon gallantly fought against has given way to the Postmodernism of our day. This tool of the forces of evil has chiseled its way to say that truth is whatever you want it to be. That giant ball of error has now become an avalanche of error. A very tiny minority of evangelicals joined Spurgeon in counterattacking the new heretics. Those who have taken the torch from the hand of the "prince of preachers" when he went to be with the Lord in 1892 are still in the minority in this the twenty first century. Unhappily these errors are a permanent part of the Christian landscape today. We who are the defenders of the faith need to look to Peter's exhortation, "Be on your guard so that you are not carried away by the error of unprincipled men and fall from your own stead-fastness, but grow in the grace and knowledge of our Lord and Savior Jesus Christ" (2 Peter 3:17–18).

In bringing this paper to a close, we have seen that unsound doctrine produces unsound living. Satan is a subtle enemy who goes about masked as an angel of light. He distorts the truth of the gospel with the evil intent of clouding our minds and stealing our hearts away from the truth as it is in Jesus. This day of ours can be called the modern day of the Judges where everyone does what is right in their own eyes. Because one is a citizen of a Christian nation, reared in a Christian home, is baptized, attends a Christian school, goes to church, and believes facts about Christianity doesn't make a person a genuine Christian as swimming in the water doesn't make one a real fish. Believing and living the truth are bound together and cannot be separated. John is not just exposing and refuting error. He takes great pains to urge upon us what we are to believe in our hearts and how we are to conduct our lives as it concerns our like precious faith. In the midst of such concerns John is showing us what it means to be a genuine Christian. He endeavors to fill us with assurance, joy, and peace in believing and living in fellowship with God and one another. Let it be the desire of our hearts that the foundational truths of historic Christianity be the anchor of our faith. Let us aim for a more consistent and faithful Christian life that will make us to be seasoning salt and bright shinning lights. Being such a spiritual condiment and beacon of truth cannot but exert a positive influence upon society in general and our immediate sphere of influence in particular. Lastly, let us look to our all powerful God to strengthen us to become bold and faithful witnesses for the truth of the gospel in this sin dark world.

John has provided three concrete tests which strip away all the false veneer of professed Christianity. Three fool proof tests which fiery flame will expose the fool's gold of a name only Christianity. Let us honestly and prayerfully appraise what we believe and how we live by the light of these God given tests. Pray that the Spirit of the Lord move us to examine ourselves and determine if we are truly standing firm in the Faith. I urge you to test yourself. It is my prayer to God that He will be pleased to use His precious Word to transform our minds and hearts in truth, love, and righteousness, to the praise of His most glorious name. Amen

SPEAK COMFORT TO ME JACOB

1 Thessalonians 4:13–18

I n Charles Dickens famous story, A Christmas Carol, we find mean miserable Ebenezer Scrooge confronted by the ghost of his former business partner, Jacob Marley. The dreadful apparition is all business as he relates his hapless fate to Scrooge. Marley is doomed to wander the earth wearing the chain he forged in life. He warns that this same terrible doom awaits Scrooge also if he continues in his self serving ways. Falling on his knees, a trembling Scrooge imploringly cries out, "Speak comfort to me Jacob." The ghastly ghost coldly replies, "I have none to give." Without doubt, mankind's most feared reality and what the Bible calls our last enemy is death. When death strikes down a friend, neighbor, co-worker, relative, or a dearly loved one people will experience a wide range of emotional responses. There can be sheer shock, numbing disbelief, acute anger, great grief, deep depression, confusion, anxiety, and feelings of hopelessness and helplessness. As people seek comfort in the aftermath of death alas the spirit of the world in offering such solace is like that of old Marley. It has none to give. When a so called Christian minister says that the dearly departed is happy in heaven playing poker or out fishing, we hear afresh the words of old Marley. When a psychic tells her clients that she has contacted their loved one who wants friends and relatives to know all is well, we hear afresh the words of old Marley. When a terrorist commits an act of murder thinking it will reward him with a seat at the right hand of his god, we hear afresh the words of old Marley. When people die who have not trusted Jesus Christ alone as their Savior from sin and Lord of their life and we are told that they are in the bliss of God's holy heaven, we hear afresh the words of old Marley. These are some of the sugar coated lies, false hope, and empty comfort that people are given when death claims its victims and ushers them into eternity. Such people are uninformed (ignorant) about so serious a matter. Outside of the Christian's Blessed Hope, the Lord Jesus Christ, His glorious Person, Word, and Work there is no genuine hope and no meaningful comfort to sooth anxious thoughts and steady wavering hearts in the aftermath of death's destructive visitation.

Coming to our text, we have a situation in the newly established church at Thessalonica in which the apostle Paul writes both to instruct and comfort believers who are sorrowing over their deceased friends and loved ones. "But we do not want you to be uniformed, brethren, about those who are asleep, so that you will not grieve as do the rest who have no hope" (vs. 13). The ancient world used sleep as a synonym for death. Such a "peaceful" word was employed to soften the terror of this grim reality. The Bible also equates sleep with death but in a transformed way as we shall see. First we ask, "Why were the Thessalonians troubled over the state of their deceased brethren?" We note that these believers recently emerged out of the muck of paganism. Paul says that they "turned to God from idols to serve a living and true God, and to wait for His Son from heaven, whom He raised from the dead, that is Jesus, who rescues us from the wrath to come" (1:9–10). The apostle had been instructing them on a number of issues such as the nature of the second coming of Jesus but had to leave Thessalonica rather quickly. This was due to pressing persecution (Acts 17:1–9; I Thessalonians 2:14–18). Paul was not able to complete his instruction. In the meanwhile some of the brethren passed away. Some may have died in the very persecution that they were experiencing (2 Thessalonians 1:4–5). The Thessalonians lack of knowledge concerning the status of those who died caused anxiety. They were concerned about what would become of the departed believers when the Lord returns. Would they be at some disadvantage? Would they see the Lord's coming in power and great glory? Would these deceased brethren miss out in some way on the glories and blessings of the second coming? There was the possible danger that the grief the Thessalonians were having might turn into despair, even the kind of despair experienced by those "who have no hope."

We read in Ephesians 2:12 that all who are outside of saving union with Jesus Christ are characterized as "having no hope and without God in the world." This hopeless world both then and now through its philosophies, cults, and religions offered no sound basis for hope and provided no real comfort concerning death and the afterlife. Back in my college days I took several classes in ancient Greek and Roman civilization. Touching the subject of death, the general thought was that when someone died their "vital breath" or soul left its "prison house" or body to enter a place known as Hades. This dreary realm was thought to be a vague and shadowy place where one existed as a phantom. As such one was perceptible but untouchable. In this place the dead lamented their existence. How depressing. Moreover, if someone did not receive a proper funeral they had to wander along the banks of the river Styx for one hundred years before they could be allowed to cross over to the other side or netherworld. The closest thought of a paradise was the Elysian Fields. This was supposed to be an island of sunshine, refreshing breezes, and lovely fragrant flowers. It was reserved at the discretion of the gods for heroes only. The select few would sing, dance, and enjoy athletic games. As people faced the eventuality of death these beliefs carried no concrete confidence, provided little or no satisfaction, and imparted a fleeting comfort at best.

Turning to more recent times, I recall a discussion several people were having on a web site which sponsored observations and thoughts on the subject of death. There was a young woman whose dear mother passed away at the relatively early age of twenty-eight. She remembered her mom as a loving, kind, intelligent, fun, and hands-on. Her mother enjoyed life taking an interest in many things. In the prime of her life, the mother unexpectedly suffered a stroke, became blind, and that former zeal for life quickly came to a halt as she rapidly faded away in mind and body. All her daughter kept saying was how unfair it was for mom to have life end in such a terrible way. Where was the justice? Where was this loving God she supposedly trusted? Why did He take her this way? Why couldn't she go peaceably? A friend came to the wake to express her pain and sorrow. This friend could only say that concerning such things there is nothing you can do. Just try to comfort one another. This friend is a "comforter" who throws up their hands as it were in despair, resigned to cold fate, and providing no real comfort at all. It is the ghost of old Marley again saying. "I have none [comfort] to give." These thoughts we have touched upon past and present only fed fear, harbored anxiety, lacked comfort, provided a shallow or false hope, and turned people's grief into despair.

The deceased Christian brethren weren't wandering along a gloomy pagan riverbank awaiting passage to "the other side." The vast majority weren't bemoaning their existence in some dreary dreamlike nether world. The select few weren't engaged in carnal delights on some island of pleasure. They weren't abandoned by God. No. The Christian faithful departed this life to "be with Christ" (Philippians 1:23). The believers were "absence from the body [. . .] at home with the Lord" (2 Corinthians 5:8). They were in the best place of all. They were safe in the arms of Jesus in heaven. This blessed reality is what we should focus on when believers depart from this side of eternity. Now we must remember that Christians do grieve. It is only natural to feel various levels of sorrow over those who leave us and are especially dear to us. I think of the wife, children, family, and friends of a brother in the Lord killed in the terrorist attack on 9/11. I recall the passing of a dear faithful brother's Christian wife of 50 years. It is not wrong nor is it improper to experience grief, even intense grief. Consider the raising of Lazarus found in John 11. Martha and Mary are grieving over the death of their brother Lazarus. Friends, family, and neighbors are at the house consoling the sisters, sharing their grief. Four days later Jesus, a beloved friend of the family, enters the village. Martha goes out to meet Jesus. Her first words to the Lord are, "Lord, if You had been here, my brother would not have died." A short while passes and Mary comes to Jesus. Falling at His feet, she says the same words to the Lord. Do you not feel the great grief of the sisters? What about Jesus? He too felt deep sorrow. "When therefore Jesus saw her weeping, and the Jews who came with her also weeping, He was *deeply moved in spirit and was troubled* [. . .] *Jesus wept* [. . .] So the Jews were saying, "See how He loved Him!" (see John 11, italics mine). Concerning the martyrdom of the godly Steven, we read, "Devout men buried Steven, and made *loud lamentation* over him" (Acts 8:2, italics mine). Friends, it is normal to grieve. But grief that is not under girded by Him who is the way, the truth, and the life (John 14:6), who is our merciful and faithful high priest (Hebrews 2:17), who is more than able to sympathize with our weaknesses (Hebrews 4:15), who is the God of hope (Romans 15:13), and who is the God of all comfort (2 Corinthians 1:3) is a hard grief to bear indeed. I have found that it is good for us to express our thoughts and feelings. If we are grieving it is not healthy to suppress it. When we "bottle up" our grief it will make it much harder to bear. It is good consolation for mind and body to express our sorrow. The apostle is not trying to put a lid on grief. It is good to tell Jesus. As the hymn writer puts it, "What a friend we have in Jesus, all our sins and grief(s) to bear." Tell your brothers and sisters in Christ. Not only are we exhorted to rejoice with those who rejoice but we are to weep with those who weep (Roman 12:15). Moreover, what the apostle does to ward off grief so that it doesn't turn into despair is to give right instruction. Over against the false hope and unsatisfying comfort found in the world's spin of the matter, Paul begins by laying down the firm foundation for genuine consolation when Christians leave for that "sweet and blessed country to that dear land of rest."

The apostle begins by calling attention to three gospel certainties. "For if we believe that Jesus died and rose again, even so God will bring with Him those who have fallen asleep in Jesus" (vs. 14). The Christian's sure and blessed hope is riveted upon the foundation of three absolute truths: Christ's atoning death for His people, His victorious resurrection, and His triumphant return. Each of these gospel verities are like the legs of a tripod. A large telescope cannot stay level and balanced if one of the tripod legs is missing or altered. It will come crashing down and be badly damaged. Take away or alter just one of these absolute truths of the gospel and the spiritual damage that occurs will be staggering. Just look at the state of many churches today as the gospel has been distorted by "progressive" thinkers. In this "lets not offend anyone" and "do away with absolutes" climate, let us thank God He has His seven thousand, "all the knees who have not bowed to Baal and every mouth that has not kissed him" (1 Kings 19:18). These are the ones who remain faithful to the old paths. Mark it concerning the absolute truth of God's Word, "To the law and to the testimony! If they do not speak according to this word, it is because they have no dawn" (Isaiah 8:20). If we believe, that is, accept without question these truths to be genuine and indisputable, we begin on sure footing. However, to believe doesn't end with knowing facts. The Scripture declares that even the demons believe that God is one (see James 2:19). The evil spirits believe who Jesus is. Mark 1:24 records their acknowledgement, "I know who You are - the Holy One of God!" and again in chapter 5 verse 7, "[. . .] Jesus, Son of the Most high God [. . .]." Satan, that arch enemy of all righteousness and father of lies knows Scripture as well (Matthew 4:5–7; Luke 4:9–12). To believe is much more than simply giving credence to Biblical facts, having the right words, and the right names. I once read somewhere a keen observation made by a Christian college professor who said, "The Bible never considers a truth to be known until it changes the life of the one who hears it."

In my witness to an unsaved friend, I laid out the gospel in its simplest terms. I literally laid before him the ABC's of the gospel: Admit you are a sinner. Believe that Jesus Christ died for you. Call upon Him as Savior and Lord. Over the course of our conversations I went into greater detail to bring out the full implications of the gospel ABC's. He keeps saying he believes but it ends there. My friend has not yet trusted Christ alone for salvation. I continue to pray for him and emphasize the need to exercise "repentance toward God and faith [belief] in our Lord Jesus Christ" (Acts 20:21). To believe facts about the gospel without these three essential certainties stirring and changing one's heart to see the glory of God in the face of Jesus Christ is a great tragedy. Such glory when it illuminates a person's mind and heart with the splendor of Christ's Person and His sacrificial love on behalf of guilty sinners so that individual gives their whole self to Him in faith, love, obedience, and service is a most glorious blessing. Not doing so again is the great tragedy. Just how many church goers, good people, moral people, and religious people are out there who simply give credence to gospel facts, words, and names yet remain strangers to saving grace? When the absolute truths of Christ's death, resurrection, and coming again are actually believed and relied upon it will impact, transform, and direct an individual's life to the service and glory of God.

When we see the battered body of the holy sinless Son of God nailed upon Calvary's cruel cross suffering and dying for my sins which were placed upon Him. When we realize that He bore the penalty for my sins which I justly deserved. When we hear His anguishing cry of abandonment amidst the darkness shrouding the landscape, "My God, My God, Why have You forsaken Me" (see Mark 15:34)? When we understand that the Lord of glory was experiencing in His body and soul the outer darkness and torments of hell which were for my sins. When we see the powerful cords of death powerless because they cannot hold Him and He rises victoriously from the grave on the third day. We hear Him declared "the Son of God with power by the resurrection from the dead, according to the Spirit of holiness, Jesus Christ our Lord" (Romans 1:4). We grasp the blessed truth that He has conquered sin, Satan, and death and is alive forever more. That God the Father has accepted as complete His perfect sacrifice for the sins of His people. When these truths grip us of the self sacrificing love of the Son of God for guilty sinners such as ourselves, it will move us to plead for mercy like the tax collector. We will then beat our breast, a picture of a broken and contrite heart that God will not despise (Psalm 51:17), calling upon God to "be merciful to me the sinner" (Luke 18:13). Not mere belief in Christian facts, words, and names but a genuine belief which results in action, in a transformed life, a new life that sees the glory of Jesus Christ. "Jesus the name that charms our fears, that bids our sorrows cease; 'tis music in the sinner's ears, 'tis life, and health, and peace. He breaks the power of reigning sin, He sets the prisoner free; His blood can make the foulest clean, His blood availed for me" (Charles Wesley, 1739).

Based on these two gospel certainties there follows a third, the Lord's return in power and great glory. Paul writes, "Even so God will bring with Him those who have fallen asleep in Jesus." Salvation brings us into blessed union with Jesus Christ. Nothing, including death can sever that union no matter who, what, or where (Romans 8:38–39). Believers who die fall asleep in Jesus. Because of what Christ has accomplished by His death and resurrection, the death of His people has been transformed into sleep. They are cradled in the loving arms of Jesus. The Puritan commentator Matthew Henry wrote,

> Death does not annihilate them. It is but a sleep to them. It is their rest, their undisturbed rest. They have retired out of this troublesome world, to rest from all their labors and sorrows, and they sleep in Jesus. Being still in union with Him, they sleep in His arms and are under His special care and protection. Their souls are in His presence, and their dust is under His care and power, so that they are not lost, nor are they losers, but great gainers by death, and their removal out of this world is into a better. [4]

Death brings believers into the immediate presence of the Lord where they live and reign with Him in the bliss of heaven (Philippians 1:23; Revelation 20:4). In that most holy and blissful place they await the final consummation of the age when Christ returns with them to worship, reign, and enjoy forever the new heavens and earth in which righteousness dwells (2 Peter 3:13).

Up to this point Paul has assured the Thessalonians they need not be anxious about those who die in the Lord. The gospel verities concerning Jesus death and resurrection are the guarantee that He is coming again with those who sleep in Him. Now Paul will describe in detail what will take place with respect to both the dead and living saints at His return. Again we note that Paul is going to do so by giving right direction. It will be according to the sure word of the Lord. The basis for this instruction is not the apostle's ideas, views, philosophy, or reason nor that of other "voices." Truth is always the best buckler in all matters. It is God's Word of truth that radiates with authority. It pours forth pure light putting all doubt and anxiety to rest. We can take the Lord's word to the bank so to speak and confidently cash the check. "For this we say to you by the word of the Lord" (vs. 15). A prophet may have related this word to Paul. The apostle himself may have received this revelation directly from the Lord. More likely this is a word of Jesus Himself which was not recorded and part of the oral tradition of the early church. Note such passages as John 20:30, 21:25, Acts 1:3, 20:35.

Paul continues his instruction, "that we who are alive and remain until the coming of the Lord, will not precede those who have fallen asleep." We learn that the living believers will have no advantage over the dearly departed ones. The later will partake of the full blessings and glory of this momentous event. "For the Lord Himself will descend from heaven with a shout, with the voice of the archangel, and with the trumpet of God; and the dead in Christ shall rise first" (vs. 16). This reliable word assures us that when our Lord returns the first thing to happen with respect to believers is that those who have died will rise first. Paul goes on to describe that event in vivid language. Keep in mind as we consider this description that because Jesus died, was buried, rose again, and ascended to the Father's Right hand, at the appointed time of the end Jesus will return to the earth as the triumphant King (Mark 13:32–37). He descends in His heavenly "chariot," the clouds of heaven (Matthew 24:30–31, Revelation 1:7). He descends just as He was seen ascending into heaven (Acts 1:11). Notice that His coming is both personal and visible. Paul tells us that the Lord's return is marked by three separate, mighty, and audible sounds. There is a shout, a voice, and a trumpet call. These expressions are charged with absolute authority, filled with great urgency, and command sheer irresistibility. First we have the shout or cry of command. Here we picture a commander giving the authoritative order for his troops to advance in battle. Consider the very vibrant picture given us in Revelation 19:11–16 of Christ's return as He leads the armies of heaven. Next is the voice of the archangel. The angels are God's ministering spirits as Hebrews 1:14 remind us. They stand in God's presence. The angels carry out God's commands. The angelic host assists, protects, and delivers God's people. Here the archangel is God's mighty messenger leading the other angels in doing God's bidding in the great events of the end. Jesus will "send forth His angels" (see Matthew 13:41–43). Then there is the trumpet of God. This is the instrument which sounds the call summoning the entire world to draw near for judgment. We see the picture in Matthew 24:30–31,

> And then the sign of the Son of Man will appear in the sky, and then all the tribes of the earth will mourn, and they will see the Son of Man coming on the clouds of the sky with power and great glory. And He will send forth His angels with a great trumpet and they will gather together His elect from the four winds, from one end of the sky to the other.

At this great summoning we read, "[. . .] and the dead in Christ will rise first. Then we who are alive and remain will be caught up together with them in the clouds to meet the Lord in the air [. . .]" (vs.16–17). I call your attention once again to the personal, visible, and audible characteristics of the Lord's glorious and triumphant return. There is not one whit of secrecy about it. A popular view of this passage has been given what can be called the "spiritual dog whistle" treatment. Those who own dogs know that these animals have very keen hearing. They hear high pitched sounds that we humans are unable to detect. Some treat this passage as if the great summons consisting of the *cry or shout* of command, the *voice* of the archangel, and the *sound* of the trumpet is like some sought of spiritual dog whistle heard only by the keen ears of believers. No! When the Lord returns He does so personally, visibly, audibly, and triumphantly. We must not lose sight of the fact that Paul is writing to comfort believers about the dearly departed saints. The unbelievers are not in view here. Note that the word "first" expresses precedence, not with regard to the unsaved but with regard to the saints. The emphasis here is on the believers. It is perfectly natural for the apostle not to mention the unbelievers. However, that the unsaved are affected is made clear by Jesus Himself. All the dead, the saved and the lost, at the appointed hour (the last day) are raised at the voice or command of the Lord (John 5:28–29). Moreover, what happens with regard to the lost is followed up by the apostle in 1 Thessalonians 5:1–11. There he addresses the question as to the time of this momentous event. A careful reading and comparing of *Scripture with Scripture* will clearly show "that day" has its reference to both the saved and unsaved. The all important questions are: Will you live together with Jesus (vs. 3)? Will that day overtake you like a thief and bring you into inescapable judgment (vs. 4–10)? Where will you be?

The apostle is exhorting and encouraging the people of God not to fear. He does not want believers to become anxious nor fret about those who die in the Lord. They will be active participants in the great events of the last day. As the souls of the dead saints are raised to be reunited with their glorified bodies, they will joyfully join their fellow brethren who will be transformed in the twinkling of an eye. Writes the apostle to the Corinthians, "Behold, I tell you a mystery; we will not all sleep, but we will all be changed, in a moment, in the twinkling of an eye, at the last trumpet; for the trumpet will sound, and the dead will be raised imperishable, and we will be changed" (1 Corinthians 15: 51–53). What a glorious reunion this will be! The people of God will be caught up together, both the living saints and those brothers and sisters who have gone before, to meet our blessed Lord in the air. To meet is an expression that has a special flavor to it. In days of old this word translated "meet" was associated with the welcoming of a dignitary on an official visit. We get the picture when the apostle Paul came to Rome (Acts 28:12–16). When the brethren heard of Paul's arrival, they came from the neighboring towns to meet the apostle and escorted him to the city. We also see this picture in Matthew 25:6–10, "But at midnight there was a shout, Behold the bridegroom! Come out to meet Him." The believers go to meet their Lord and together they go in to the heavenly wedding feast. This is something like what happens when we are gathered together to meet Jesus, our King. What a joyful moment this will be for those who have longed for His appearing. It will be the pinnacle of blessedness, the height of happiness, and the apex of fellowship with our Blessed Lord and one another.

We meet Him in the air. Why the air? The air in the physical realm is a mixture of gases which forms the atmosphere around us. Interestingly, the air contained quite a mixture of evil. It was known as the abode of evil spirits. Satan is not only the god of this world-age he is also called the prince of the power of the air (Ephesians 2:2). The air served as the evil one's staging ground. Just as the air surrounds the earth so does the forces of evil. The return of the conquering King brings the forces of evil to naught. This meeting in the air proves that nothing in all of creation and no one in the entire cosmos is more powerful than the King of kings and Lord of lords. The Lordship of Jesus Christ is supreme over all realms, spiritual and material, including the air, the very place the forces of evil once operated. The air no longer has any evil powers or influence associated with it. It is on this reclaimed "ground" that the conquerors meet. Then they will return with their Lord to judge the world (1 Corinthians 6:2; Daniel 7:18, 22, 27; Matthew 19:28). The Lord's return ushers in the age to come. The second coming of Jesus Christ is marked by resurrection, judgment, and the restoration of all things. This earth which has been cleansed from all evil and sin will be renewed and restored to

Paradise. Our eternal inheritance and eternal abode will be with our Lord in the new heavens and new earth.

As this most glorious and blessed reunion takes place together with all the great events that accompany it, the apostle tells us the wonderful result, " [. . .] and so we shall always be with the Lord." When you hear those magnificent words does it not thrill you in a blessed way? Does it not make you want to find out more about these exciting details? It is only natural that we would like to learn more but Paul has met his purpose. He stops there. Paul will have us meditate on these sure words that we shall always be with the Lord. What a magnificent thought! What a grand and glad day! What a glorious reality! We shall always be with Jesus! He Himself promises; "[. . .] and I go to prepare a place for you. If I go and prepare a place for you, I will come again and receive you to Myself, that where I am, there you may be also" (John 14:2–3). As I write I cannot but help stop to sing the hymn of Horatius Bonar (1844):

A few more years shall roll, a few more seasons come, and we shall be with those that rest asleep within the tomb.

Then, O Lord, prepare my soul for that great day.

A few more storms shall beat on this wild rocky shore, and we shall be where tempests cease, and surges swell no more.

Then, O Lord, prepare my soul for that calm day.

A few more Sabbaths here shall cheer us on our way, and we shall reach the endless rest,

the eternal Sabbath day.

Then, O Lord, prepare my soul for that sweet day.

'Tis but a little while, and He shall come again. Who died that we might live, who lives that we with Him reign.

Then, O Lord, prepare my soul for that glad day.

O wash me in Thy precious blood and take my sins away. Amen.

In light of this sure instruction and its blessed truth, the apostle concludes with the exhortation, "Therefore comfort one another with these words" (vs. 18). The spirit of the world and the Spirit of Christ stand on opposite sides of the *sure* of comfort. Sympathy has its rightful place in providing comfort for those who mourn the loss of someone who has passed away. We must not fail to offer a sympathetic ear, say a sympathetic word, and manifest a sympathetic heart toward those who sorrow over the death of others. When people die it is a popular practice today to have a service which celebrates the life of the departed individual. However, the best the spirit of the world can do is offer comforting sentiments. These impart a good feeling and perhaps a good memory or two but that's where the line is drawn. It simply does not truly satisfy or bring lasting comfort at all. It is old Marley on the scene saying, "I have none [comfort] to give." Christian comfort in order to be genuine must be framed by the truth of the gospel. Paul has instructed the Thessalonians and us that genuine, meaningful, and lasting consolation along with its counterpart hope is anchored on the absolute truth of the death, resurrection, and coming again of the Lord of Glory, Jesus Christ. When our brothers and sisters in the Lord sorrow in the aftermath of death, let us be sure we comfort them with the magnificent and most precious promises of the gospel.

As we draw this paper to a close let me ask, "Do you take comfort in the sure word of the Lord? Do you possess the genuine eternal comfort and good hope by grace?" (2 Thessalonians 2:16). This blessed comfort and hope can only be had when a person is brought by the wondrous grace of God into saving union with the Lord Jesus Christ. To do so a person must acknowledge their rebellion against God. He or she must repent (turn) from sin and self. This individual then places their entire trust in Christ alone as Savior from sin and Lord of their life. There is only one way of salvation. Jesus Christ alone is that way. He is the only door to eternal life. It is not simply a matter of raising a hand or walking an aisle when the gospel invitation is given. It is not simply saying I love or believe in Jesus. It will not suffice to say I am a good person or I go to church. It is much more than that. It is having personal dealings with Him. Where there is no personal knowledge and no practical relationship with the God of the Bible who alone is the One True Living God and only Savior, there will be no sure confidence, no sure hope, and no sure comfort in the face of life and death. Have you by the grace of God been brought into right relationship and fellowship with Him? Have you been truly sorry for your sins? Have you truly turned from your sins? Have you truly trusted the Lord Jesus Christ alone and walk obediently by faith in Him? Only then can a person have peace with God. Only then can a person stand on the sure and firm foundation of eternal hope and good comfort.

Mankind's great enemy death still lays claim to its victims. When death strikes it ushers us into eternity. Eternity is forever home to only two final places. Jesus Himself says so (see Luke 16: 19–31). Beware of those who say otherwise. Beware of those who bring another gospel. Beware of those who add or subtract from the Holy Scriptures. Be especially on the alert if they are cloaked in garments with Christian tags. Will you my friend like Lazarus be carried by the angels to Abraham's bosom? Will you my friend like the rich man find yourself in that awful place of separation from God because of your sin and rebellion against Him? Will you be with the Lord or not? Do you not see my Christian friend the utter urgency to tell others about Jesus? Do you not see how crucial it is to be a faithful witness by word and deed for the Lord? O my sinner friend, do you not see the dangerous condition you are in? We cannot change the past of those who have died not trusting the Lord. However, we can change our past in the present by the grace of God. While you are on this side of eternity thank God it is still the day of salvation. Only in Jesus will you find true rest for your soul. If you know Him not, I urge you, be reconciled to Christ. The door of salvation rests on two hinges: repentance and faith. To those of us who come to God by this door, let us rejoice in the truth that whether we are awake or asleep we will live together with Him who has conquered Satan, sin, and death. What a blessed thought—reality, hope, peace, and comfort! As we consider these things, may the Living God be pleased to give us the grace to be faithful followers, effective witnesses, and true comforters as we love, obey, and serve Him who alone is our Blessed Hope and the God of all comfort. Amen

WHAT STATE AM I IN?

A Practical Look at Psalm 1

☩

A commentator from another generation by the name of Dodd said, "The Psalms are fitted to all persons and ages, to all manner of employments, and to all conditions and circumstances of life."[5] With this comment in mind, we begin this paper on Psalm 1 by stating that the Word of God divides the human race into two groups: those in the state of nature and those in the state of grace (Ephesians 2:1–10). The first group is the unsaved. They are further described in the Bible as the lost, wicked, weeds, goats, sinners, unrighteous, ungodly, and children of the devil. These are by nature spiritually dead, separated from God, walking the wide road that leads to destruction, and are the servants of Satan, sin, and self. The later group is the saved. They are further described as the godly, wheat, sheep, righteous, saints, and children of God. These by the grace of God (His unmerited favor toward sinners) are made spiritually alive in Christ, restored to fellowship with God, adopted into His family, walking the narrow road that leads to life, and serve their Savior and Lord in newness of life. Every person is found in one of these two conditions. There is no in between state. There is no neutral ground. As we walk the road of life, let us stop a moment and ask ourselves,

"What state am I in?" Am I in the state of nature which finds me dead in sin? Or am I in the state of grace which finds me alive in Christ? How can I know? To find out, our measuring stick is God's unerring Word, the Bible. Our calibration mark is Psalm 1. Let us see how we measure up. The reformer and pastor of Geneva, John Calvin, called the Psalms "an anatomy of the soul."⁶ Anatomy by definition means the fabric, make-up, or constituent structure of something. Psalm 1 shows us the different character and condition, the anatomy if you will, of those in these two states.

The psalmist begins by pronouncing a blessing upon the godly person (vs.1). Blessedness is a condition of happiness, prosperity, or contentment. I often hear people say how blessed they are to live in America. To enjoy the many freedoms found here. This country offers them the chance to live the "American Dream." To live in a land that provides the opportunity for "life, liberty, and the pursuit of happiness." However, blessedness is not a condition confined to the physical sphere alone. It is found in the spiritual realm also. The godly, because they know the Lord and walk in fellowship with Him, will find themselves in a condition of blessedness. Such a state is further determined by what the saved person avoids and embraces in life. The godly have a new way of living or to use a common term, a new lifestyle. A lifestyle is a reflection of a person's preferences and values. It is a manner of living framed by how a person thinks and acts. The psalmist proceeds to set the godly man's conduct over against that of the ungodly. There are three synonyms employed to describe the ungodly: the wicked, sinners, and scoffers. Each has their own distinct way of rebelling against God. Each of these ways the godly seeks to avoid as they follow the Lord on their course through this world.

The state of blessedness manifests itself when the godly person "walks not in the counsel of the wicked." To walk is a biblical metaphor for how a person lives their life. A saved person walks by faith in the Lord Jesus Christ alone. Because he or she is a new creation, this new life is rooted in a new purpose for living. This new life also is attended by a new focal point of concern. The saved person now lives not to please self but God. They set their desire on spiritual and eternal things as opposed to earthly and temporal things. As a result, the godly person, having these new principles embedded in the heart, seeks to avoid the counsel of the wicked. The believer endeavors by the grace of God not to live according to the advice, ideals, aims, principles, conduct, and philosophies of the unsaved. Granted, not all the counsel of the unsaved is necessarily evil. A doctor, financial advisor, or a personal trainer, who doesn't know the Lord, can offer sound counsel to improve a person's situation or well being. There is a danger though. We live in a fallen sin cursed world. Because we rub shoulders with the unsaved in the everyday affairs of life, Christians need to exercise caution when encountering the counsel of unbelievers. It literally surrounds us like the atmosphere. Before we make a decision and pursue a course of action we must bring what we see, read, or hear to the light of God's Word. Our final decision must be, "What do the Scriptures say?" We must submit our entire person, mind and body, to the Lordship of Jesus Christ. What would Jesus do? Intermingled with good counsel there is much that is bad. Unsound counsel is geared to exploit us. Its intent is to sway us away from God and the principles of His Word. Every area of life is subjected to unbiblical counsel. It is ever ready to steal our affections away from God and compromise our loyalty to Christ. The mass media in all its venues: television, radio, books, music, movies, seminars, magazines, newspapers, and the many headed monster of the internet is jam packed with such counsel. One needs to wield a spiritual machete to chop their way through the tangling overgrowth of ungodly ways and means offered to all regardless of age, race, creed, and station in life. Beware. The counsel of the wicked comes to us like the Siren voices of mythological lore. These seductive sweet singing creatures would captivate the eyes and ears of sailors and lure them to shipwreck and destruction.

When we turn on the television, tune in the radio, pop in a CD, go "on line," visit our local library, news stand, or bookstore we will find an entire philosophy of life at our disposal. Much that permeates the mass media is contrary to the Christian world view and manner of living. This is not to knock all television or radio programs. Nor am I bashing the internet, libraries, or bookstores. I like to surf the aisles, thumb through magazines that interest me, or go on select websites that I find helpful. I enjoy an informative nature, history, biography, science program, or website, especially a Christian one. However, we still need to be careful and exercise sanctified common sense. This is especially true when we come across self-help books by the world's experts, the powerful message in music, the advice of "media" psychologists, talk show chatter, catchy ads, "entertaining" sitcoms, movies, videos, plays, reality shows, and the like. We must treat them with utmost caution. Some of these things Christians should not even think of entertaining. Far too much that is directed at our senses is intended by the enemies of righteousness to sway our way of thinking and living that is not God centered, honoring, and glorifying. Those who hold allegiance to Jesus Christ as Lord must seek divine grace and guidance to follow the principle laid down for us by the apostle in Philippians 4:8. Mark the descriptive terms that Paul uses, "Finally brethren, whatever is true, whatever is honorable, whatever is right, whatever is pure, whatever is lovely, whatever is of good repute, if there is any excellence, and if anything worthy of praise, dwell [ponder] on these things." These wonderful virtues are to be sought out and treasured by those who know and love the truth. A Christian brother once suggested to me concerning the reading of Bible commentaries what he called the "spiritual eating approach."

When reading he recommended doing so as if eating a piece of fish. Eat and enjoy the meat but be sure to quickly spit out the bones. Such an approach is commendable for any book or form of the media, even Christian ones. How about our approach to the world and its anti-Christian viewpoint and lifestyle? The apostle John is very clear in his direction for us. He writes in 1 John 2:15–17,

> Do not love the world nor the things in the world. If anyone loves the world, the love of the Father is not in him [or her]. For all that is in the world, the lust of the flesh and the lust of the eyes and the boastful pride [proud display] of life, is not from the Father, but is from the world. The world is passing away, and also its lusts; but the one who does the will of God lives forever.

This world that we are forbidden to love is what A.W. Pink calls, "Fallen human nature acting itself out in the human family [. . .] the organized kingdom of the 'carnal mind' which is 'enmity (hostility) against God' and which is 'not subject to the Law of God, neither indeed can be'7 (Romans 8:7). In short worldliness is the world without God. Worldly things are temporary and fleeting. The apostle is warning believers never to flirt or compromise with the spirit of this evil world-age. Never are we to adopt a worldly lifestyle. God's people are to be in the world as the followers and witness of the Lord Jesus but not to participate in its system of thinking and living that is contrary to the revealed will of God. James warns us about being friends with this world. Friendship involves trust and affection. The world system is not the friend of the Christian. It is not our ally. This world does not support or help the Christian in any way as a true friend would. Such friendship is nothing less than hostility toward God. Such friendship makes a person an enemy of God (see James 4:4). Yet there are those who have forged friendships with the world system because of sheer carelessness or neglect of their Christian duties (e.g. Bible study and prayer). Such find themselves entangled in the sticky web of worldliness. Be careful who and what you trust. Be careful who and what vies for your affection.

How many professing Christians have fallen captive to the Siren voices of the wicked? How many are flirting with danger? How many have made shipwreck of the Faith? How much are we like the world as it pertains to our lifestyle? Can the unsaved see anything different about Christians? If anyone heeds the counsel of the wicked they shall surely grieve the Holy Spirit who is our true Counselor. Let us remember that the counsel of the wicked comes to us like Bunyan's Mr. Worldly Wiseman. This sly fellow succeeds in deceiving Christian with his seemingly sound advice. Evangelist finds Christian at a standstill. He then calls attention to Christian's folly for taking Mr. Worldly Wiseman's advice. Evangelist begins to correct Christian: "Now there are three things in this man's counsel that thou must utterly abhor. 1) His turning thee out of the Way. 2) His laboring to make the Cross odious to thee. 3) And his setting thy feet in the way that leadeth unto the administration of death."[8] The simple tinker, fine preacher, and puritan divine, John Bunyan wrote his Pilgrim's Progress from a prison cell in the sixteen hundreds. Who can deny that he still has his finger on the spiritual pulse even of our generation? Mark it. The counsel of the wicked spares no pains to lead us away from Christ's glorious Person, Word, and Work. It labors tirelessly to undermine our living lives of "godliness and dignity." It goes to great lengths to prevent us from listening to the good counsel of God which by His grace is "instructing us to deny ungodliness and worldly desires and to live sensibly, righteously, and godly in the present [evil] age, looking for the blessed hope and the appearing of the glory of our great God and Savior, Christ Jesus" (Titus 2:12–14). The world's sages are very vocal, unashamed in their boldness, and dangerously subtle as they offer us their unholy wares. Let us be careful what we watch, listen to, and read. Our eyes and ears are bombarded with violence, greed, sexual immorality, sensuality, hate, revenge, racial prejudice, living for the moment, cheating, lying, dirty language, the taking of God's name frivolously, arrogance, slander, criticism, defying authority, self importance, the glitter of worldliness, and the glare of materialism. These unholy things are being promoted from many quarters as good, normal, fun, and even entertaining. No. The godly person seeks by the grace of God to turn away from the counsel of the wicked in all its sizes, shapes, colors, and hues.

In the next place the Psalmist says the godly person does not stand in the path of sinners. To stand means to maintain one's cause. During the Texas war for independence from Mexico in 1836, the defenders of the Alamo took a stand against the advancing Mexican army. I recall my dad telling us about the Battle of the Bulge during the Second World War. At the town of Bastogne in Belgium, the heavily outnumbered allies took a stand against the unexpected advancing German army. These soldiers stood in a path that spelled defiance. Sinners do the same when it comes to standing on holy ground. Psalm 2 reminds us that sinners take a stand against the Lord and his Anointed (Christ). The apostles cite part of this Psalm in their prayer for boldness in their witness for the cause of Christ. They call attention to the opposition the Lord Jesus and they themselves faced from Jew and Gentile alike. We look again to Bunyan's pilgrim as Christian is confronted in the Way by the evil Apollyon. "Then Apollyon broke out into a grievous rage, saying, I am an enemy to this Prince. I hate his person, his laws, and his people: I am come out on purpose to withstand thee."[9] Like their master the devil, sinners go and do the same. They defy God and His people by taking a stand against all righteousness. The godly will always be assaulted by Satan and his evil cohorts. Jesus and his apostles tell us so. "Be of sober spirit, be on the alert. Your adversary, the devil, prowls around like a roaring lion, seeking someone to devour" (1 Peter 5:8). "In the world you have tribulation" (John 16:33). "Through many tribulations we must enter the kingdom of God" (Acts 14:22). "Indeed, all who desire to live godly in Christ Jesus will be persecuted" (2 Timothy 3:12). How then do we counter the enemies of righteousness? We do so by putting on the full armor of God as Paul exhort us to do in Ephesians 6:10–18. We note in particular verse 17. We are urged to wield the sword of the Spirit, which is the Word of God. Like Jesus we should meet the suggestions of evil head on with, "On the other hand it is written in the Scriptures" (Matthew 4:7). Furthermore we must use this all important weapon along with what I'm calling a "heaven-ward mental reorientation." Orientation basically means the direction something lies in, is developed, or focused upon. When a student is attending college for the first time, the institution provides a "freshman orientation" to help the individual adjust to the new setting. New workers too are offered "job orientation" to help them get better acquainted with their new position. The orientation of the counsel of the wicked is downward, earthly, and opposed to God. Christians are confronted by such unspiritual and unholy orientation twenty four hours a day and seven days a week. There is no let up. Reorientation means to find out where we are, where we are going, and to change direction where needs be. The word of God always steers us in the right direction so that we will not only think right but act right. Paul reminds Christians to keep seeking the things above and to be intent on them (see Colossians 3:1–2). This mental reorientation in the things of God together with a diligent "watching and praying" will enable us to keep from stumbling over the obstacles placed in our path by sinners.

The third way the saved person finds them self in a condition of blessedness is when he or she sits not in the seat of scoffers. A scoffer is a person who holds up the nose in derision at someone or something. The Jewish religious leaders scoffed at our Lord and His teaching. They derided him as he hung dying on the cross for our sins. The Athenian sages scoffed at Paul as he preached and reasoned with them on Mars Hill. The scoffer makes a mockery of all that is holy, righteous, and good. In the parable of the marriage feast we find two negative reactions to the gospel: indifference and hostility (see Matthew 22:1–14). Both scoff at the things of God. Those who make light of the good news brush aside the gospel invitation as unimportant (vs. 5). They have other and more seemingly relevant things to do. Those who are hostile to the gospel are more animate in their mockery (vs.6). You're a fanatic. Shut up! Don't talk to me about Christ, sin, repentance, or faith. These disrespect, mistreat, and even slay the people of God. Sitting was the more common posture of a teacher. The scoffer sits down in his easy chair of sin. He mocks the way the godly think and live. He teaches others his own wicked thoughts and ways. We look once more to Bunyan's immortal Pilgrim's Progress. We see an entire jury made up of scoffers at the trial of Faithful. There is Mr.'s Blind-man, No-good, Malice, Love-lust, Live-loose, Heady, High-Mind, Enmity, Liar, Cruelty, Hate-light, and Implacable. The very titles of these unrighteous jurors speak volumes as to the content and extent of their scoffing. These members of the evil jury that sit in examination of the faithful and godly followers of the Lord are still with us today. They park themselves everywhere in the stations of life. Beware of those who despise God, his ways, and his people. The blessed person does not take a seat with them nor gives countenance to their evil machinations. Blessed is the person who avoids the seat of scoffers, the path of sinners, and the counsel of the wicked.

Next the Psalmist takes up the positive aspect of the godly person's lifestyle (vs.2). The godly embrace the Law of the Lord. This is achieved by a two-fold action. They delight and meditate in that Law. The dictionary defines law as a rule of action or conduct established by authority, society, and custom. The majority of laws are intended for good. Laws are necessary otherwise society would be ruled by chaos and anarchy. Thomas Jefferson said, "Where law ends, tyranny begins." History is littered with the wrecks of those who have misused law for their own self serving purposes. Aside from the abuse of law, can you imagine what it would be like if we did not have laws addressing how our government operates (e.g. the system of checks and balances)? Or traffic, fire safety, environmental, investment, and all the other laws that are part and parcel of every day life? It is unthinkable what society would be like or how long it would last. To be sure some laws are bad and downright evil (e.g. abortion.) These need to be replaced or amended for the betterment of all. However, in general law is a good thing for society to have in place. Here in vs. 2 we have the Law of laws. This Law is holy, righteous, and good. It carries with it both temporal and eternal ramifications. It is the Law established by the Living God who alone is the Blessed and only Sovereign. This most excellent law is the Law of the Lord.

The Hebrew word translated law is Torah. It is used 220 times in the Old Testament. Torah can also mean instruction or direction. This Law however must not be limited to a portion of Scripture. As Calvin rightly observes, "When David speaks here of the Law, it ought not to be understood as if other parts of Scripture should be excluded but rather, since the whole of Scripture is nothing else than the exposition of the Law, under it as the head is comprehended the whole body."[10] Therefore, the will of God which is expressed in His words, precepts, and actions are his Torah (law, direction, instruction) for us. A good practice for every church is to incorporate the systematic reading of the Word of God in its worship service. This is not simply my idea. The apostle Paul exhorts young Pastor Timothy to "give attention to the public reading of Scripture, to exhortation and teaching" (1 Timothy 4:13). One church I attended had a portion of the New Testament read during the morning worship service and the Old

Testament at the evening service. Another church had as part of its service, "God's Will for Our Lives." The pastor would read from week to week the Ten Commandments or a practical portion of Scripture such as Romans 12, Colossians 3, or a segment of Psalm 119.

The Ten Commandments are the moral Law of God which is binding upon all mankind. The practical portions of Scripture are the out workings of that Law. All the commandments and exhortations of Scripture show us the why and how we are to live before God and our fellow man. As our King, the Lord Jesus rules over us by giving us laws which we are to conform our minds, hearts, and lives too (Isaiah 33: 22). The Law of the Lord should be our delight. To those who think otherwise consider our Lord Jesus Christ. The Lord Jesus delighted to do the Father's will. He explained, expanded and reinforced the Law. "You have heard that the ancients were told [. . .] but I say to you [. . .]" (see Matthew 5–7, our Lord's Sermon on the Mount). The Lord Jesus kept the Law of God perfectly, died for our sins (lawlessness), and was raised for our justification. We receive this great salvation from God as a free gift through faith. As a result we are no longer under the Law as a "covenant of works" in which we seek to earn our salvation and justification before God.

During the 16th century Reformation when men returned to the Bible as the absolute truth and rule of faith (what we are to believe) and practice (how we are to live), three great Reformation principles were born: Scripture alone, Christ alone, and Faith alone. At that time the erroneous view of salvation perpetrated by Rome had been the bane of popery for centuries (and still is today). Among the first to search the Scriptures to see whether these things were so, were the forerunners of the Reformation. These inquirers included such groups from parts of Italy, Spain, and France known as the Albigenses and the Waldenses. There were also faithful men such as John Wyclif, John Huss, and Savonarola. Then Luther was raised up whose eyes

God also opened to see that sinners are saved by grace (God's unmerited favor toward sinners) through faith alone not by one's efforts or merits. (Ephesians 2:8–9) There was Calvin and Zwingli, leading the reformation in their respective countries. Hence the great doctrine of "Justification by Faith" was thundered forth. Another group zealous for the truth was the Anabaptists (which means re-baptizers). They put a strong emphasis on the practical aspects of the faith, namely following Jesus. The very first Anabaptists (more properly called the Swiss Brethren) such as Conrad Grebel, Felix Manz, and George Blaurock, right from the start believed that the teaching and commandments of the Lord were given to be put into practice. The pivotal doctrine of justification by faith alone didn't stop there for them. The Anabaptists who devoted themselves to the Scriptures, although misunderstood, maligned, and severely persecuted by Catholics and Protestants alike for their "radical" views (e.g. believers baptism, non violence, separation of church and state) endeavored to obey the Lord not to gain favor with God. They strove to be faithful to walk as Jesus walked. They took the teachings of Jesus at face value and sought to obey them. These brethren sought to be faithful in their witness for the gospel by word and deed. This helps underscore the truth that we are to "prove ourselves doers of the word, and not merely hearers who delude themselves" (James 1:22). It is the effectual doer of the Word who will be blessed in what he does (James 1:25).

A person's actions do speak louder than their words. They will reflect what we believe. When God saves us we become a new creation. The old things pass away. The new comes. The apostle is clear about that in 2 Corinthians 5:17. God restores us to a right relationship and renewed fellowship with Himself. In doing this God doesn't eliminate our obligation as His responsible moral creatures to obey Him. The Law of the Lord, embodied in His Holy Word, is now for us *a rule of life* as it directs us in our walk by faith in Christ alone. It instructs us in the will and ways of our Sovereign God. As the familiar hymn of James Sammis says, "Trust and obey, for there is no other way. To be happy in Jesus, but to trust and obey." This should ever be the believers delight.

To delight means that which brings great joy and happiness. Everyone has something they enjoy in a special way. I enjoy nature and history. I delight in the wonders of creation when I go hiking, tend my gardens, take nature photos, or stargaze with my telescope. I find the history of people, places, and things interesting. Others enjoy painting, making crafts, visiting museums, writing poetry, art, woodworking, coin collecting, fishing, playing a musical instrument, reading mystery novels, sewing, or restoring old cars. There is nothing wrong with enjoying our hobbies. It is good for Christians to do so. Our interests and hobbies can be used as opportunities for fellowship and witness. You can form a sewing group, a book club, or use the wonders of nature as a springboard to tell others about our great God and Savior. Now let us reason together. Don't we have to set aside time for these good things? Of course we do. What about the Word of God? Is this not the Book we Christians believe and obey? What place does it hold in the things that delight us? God's Word ought to be our foremost delight. It is the living and enduring Word of God, the guiding light that shines in the darkness of a sin laden world, and the only stable foundation for all things that pertain to life and godliness (1 Peter 1:25; 2 Peter 1:3–4, 19). Are we setting aside the proper amount of time for the Word of the Lord? Oh how sweet and precious the Bible should be to every believer. Those in the state of grace are ruled by the Law of the Lord. Again we emphasize not as a written legal code but as Torah, as instruction and direction. Can we say with David, "I have rejoiced in the way of Your testimonies, as much as in all riches. I will meditate on Your precepts and regard Your ways. I shall delight in Your statues; I shall not forget Your word."

"Make me walk in the path of Your commandments, for I delight in it" (Psalm 119:14–16, 35).

At the back entrance to our home we have an arbor that is draped in summer with the sweet smelling aroma of wisteria. There the bees busy themselves drinking the delicious nectar. Are we bee-like Christians who busy themselves drinking the nourishment of God's Word? Is it our main delight? It is not enough to simply read our daily chapter or two being content we have done our duty. We must take time to meditate on the Word. This is essential if we are to truly profit from it. What does it mean to meditate? It is to think, to ponder, to reflect upon with a serious thoughtfulness. That household name among the Puritans, Matthew Henry writes, "To meditate in God's Word is to discourse with ourselves concerning the great things contained in it with close application and fixedness of thought."[11] No one will argue that our day is fast paced, hectic, and full of the hustle and bustle of everyday living. We have our jobs or school to attend. There are many things to do and places to go. There never seems to be enough time in the day for it all. Some people I know confess they are just too tired to take up their Bibles at times because of their work load or due to sleepless nights being up with the baby. I for one understand because I too have struggled with those same realities of life. I worked on Wall Street holding a pressure packed job selling money market instruments where I had to be mentally sharp. I had to endure the many not so pleasant and tiring rush hour commutes home. There were four children to attend to. My children when infants were not good sleepers at night. When they became older there was school and activities that demanded time as some of you soccer moms and little league dads are acquainted with. I know where others are coming from when they find themselves mentally or physically drained and being inconsistent in their personal devotions. However don't we make the time to do that which is necessary and enjoyable? Yes we do. We make sure we eat, drink, and sleep. We make sure we take our medicine if we are ill, earn a paycheck, be on time for work or a particular function, go on vacation, watch a favorite TV program, attend a ball game, a concert, or view the new art exhibit. If we can make the time for these things then we must do likewise for spiritual things. A verse of Scripture that has stuck with me from the beginning of my Christian life is, "Discipline [train] yourself for the purpose of godliness" (1 Timothy 4:7). Just as we don't deny ourselves food and drink we must not deny ourselves spiritual food and drink. If we lack either we will become weak and sickly, physically or spiritually. How many out there need to restart or readjust their spiritual training?

The sporadic or complete lack of meditation in the Word of God will eventually result in grace not flourishing as it should. Our Christian duties or priorities will eventually become burdensome. Then prayer, the very lifeblood of the Christian will become lethargic. Worship and praise will be found listless. Our witness will be stamped with ineffectiveness. If this is true or we see it beginning to happen then we must get our spiritual priorities in order. Discipline, train, exercise yourself for the purpose of godliness. Exercise together with proper nutrition goes a long way in making us feel better physically, mentally, and emotionally. The same is true in the spiritual sphere. We may need to start exercising more consistently what is rightly called the means of grace. These means are Bible study, meditation, prayer, and all the aspects associated with worship (e.g. the Lord's Supper). For some of us we may have to trim the fat so to speak. We may need to limit or eliminate some of our temporal activities in order to make room for our spiritual exercises. I'm not saying for example that all Christians should unplug their televisions. But just think of the amount of time we spend watching it. Is it too much to give up an hour of our "free" time to spend it in meditation and prayer? Be sure to start and end the day before the throne of grace in prayer. I have gotten into the practice of using my work break, a part of my lunch time, and when I am alone driving for prayer. Are we not exhorted to pray without ceasing? There is no such thing as a prayer less Christian.

Perhaps try your hand at journaling. Keep a written record of your everyday experiences. Record your thoughts, observations, and reflections about your daily life, what goes on around you, your prayers, and meditation in the Holy Scriptures. Take notes during Bible study and the sermon. That is a sure way to stay focused when listening. Then set a time in the afternoon perhaps sharing it around the Sunday mealtime table. It is a most profitable exercise to reflect upon what you've heard and apply it to your life. Be sure to make a proper use of the Lord's Day. That day was made especially for both our physical and spiritual well being. There is much truth in an old saying, "Sunday is the spiritual market day of the week. Lay in store holy thoughts and feelings. Let the first day set the tune for the whole week."[12] Use that day to delight and nourish your self in the things of God. We must delight in the Torah of the Lord and meditate in it day and night. That means frequently and diligently. When you meditate in the Word ask yourself, what is God saying to me? How should this passage make me think and act? How does it apply to my particular circumstance or situation? This is how we let the Word of Christ dwell in us. How we hide His Word in our hearts that we may not sin against Him. How we become doers of the Word to the glory of God and the good of our neighbor. David said, "The precepts of the Lord are right, rejoicing the heart" (Psalm 19:8). Jesus said, "If you love Me, you will keep My commandments" (John 14:15). The beloved apostle said, "For this is the love of God, that we keep His commandments; and His commandments are not burdensome" (1 John 5:3). Do we delight and meditate in the Law of the Lord by day? Can we say with the Psalmist, "Lead me in Your truth and teach me, for You are the God of my salvation; For You I wait all day." Do we delight and meditate in the Law of the Lord by night? "My soul is satisfied as with marrow and fatness, and my mouth offers praises with joyful lips. When I remember You on my bed, I meditate on You in the night watches" (Psalm 25:5, 63:5–6). Such does the godly person.

As a result of the godly person's lifestyle the Psalmist compares them to lush green trees planted by streams of water. I have always found trees to be interesting. Working a seasonal position as a park ranger, I had the pleasure of spending large amounts of the working day surrounded by these fascinating members of creation. I came to learn the various types that were common to the park and their different characteristics. There was the Sassafras tree with three different shaped leaves on the same branch and lemon scented twigs. Its oil is used in soaps and rubbing lotions, its fruit eaten by our winged friends, and its soft bark browsed by deer and rabbits. There was the White Oak tree with its gray bark, grayish twigs, and large acorns. Its wood is used for furniture, flooring, rail road ties, and fuel. Its fruit enjoyed by song birds, raccoons, chipmunks, and squirrels. There was the flowering Dogwood with its lovely small white flowers. These are just a sample of the beauty, uniqueness, and usefulness of trees. Are we not awed by the spectacular splashes of color in autumn? Refreshed by the breathtaking beauty of "rebirth" in the spring? Trees provide shade, protection, timber, fuel, food, and cleanse the air. Trees are indeed both useful and beautiful.

The godly are the plantings of the Lord (Matthew 15:13). Planted by divine grace, flourishing in the state of grace, living to serve and glorify God, they are like firmly planted trees, beautiful and useful in the eyes of the Lord (Isaiah 60:21; 61:3). What is it that makes a tree flourish? Someone has rightly said, "Where there is water there is life, where water is scarce life is a struggle." The Bible paints a very vivid picture of the devastating effects of drought on all forms of life

(Jeremiah 14:1–6 and 1 Kings 17–18). You may recall in your school studies the famous Dust Bowl which adversely affected the southern Plains states from 1931–1938. The land became greatly distressed. As food became scarce, food prices went up. Many lost their farms as the drought was accompanied by terrible damaging dust storms. I remember watching news reports about the bad drought which burdened some 35 states during the 1980's. Water is indeed a precious commodity. When we send probes to other planets what is the one thing scientists are eager to find? H20. Water is essential for all life forms. In order for a tree to grow, keep lush, green, and fruitful it needs a sufficient water source.

The same holds true for the child of God in the spiritual realm. We find in Jeremiah 2:13 that God calls Himself, "The fountain of living waters." Our blessed Lord Jesus offers thirsty souls, "living water" (John 4:10). As "trees" of the Lord, He supplies His own with the living water of spiritual nourishment through His Word and by His Spirit. All that Christ is in His glorious Person and work is the well spring that supplies His people with abundant amounts of grace, mercy, and peace. Just as earthly water is essential to us in the physical realm so is "heavenly water" in the spiritual realm. This living spiritual water is cool, refreshing, cleansing, purifying, and thirst quenching to everyone who believes and walks by faith in Him. As a result, the child of God like a flourishing tree yields its fruit in season. Those in fellowship with God will bring forth a distinct harvest. Our Lord reminds us that fruit bearing is a distinguishing mark of His own. "You will know the tree [true or false believer] by their fruit" (Matthew 7:15–20; John 15:1–17). What kind of fruit do believers bring forth? A direct outcome of their manner of living yields the fruits of the Spirit and the bearing of fruit in every good work (Galatians 5:22–23; Colossians 1:10). Whether it is in times of sunshine, cloudiness, or storm in the Christian's life, these good fruits will be evident to some degree in the life of God's people. The harvest of fruit will vary from Christian to Christian. Some will bear fruit thirty, some sixty, and some a hundred fold and prove they are in saving union with the Lord (Mark 4:20; Luke 8:15). Those who avoid evil and embrace the Law of the Lord will have leaves that remain green and lush, like an evergreen all year round. Their profession of faith will not be temporary. The godly will have their ups and downs, peaks and valleys, and their share of trials and triumphs. Yet the faith of God's people will never dry out and die because their roots are firmly anchored in the rich watered soil of the wondrous grace of God. They are "the called, beloved in God the Father, and kept for Jesus Christ" (Jude 1). They are those who are "doers of the word" and "bear fruit" to the glory of God (James 1:21; John 15:8).

Furthermore, prosperity says the Psalmist, will attend the godly person. Those who diligently meditate in and obey the Torah (law, direction, instruction) of the Lord will prosper and have good success (Joshua 1:8). The world views and pursues prosperity from the perspective of fame, social standing, wealth, and material possessions. There is nothing wrong with temporal prosperity as long as it doesn't consume us to the point where we are slack concerning the things of God. We must beware of having an inordinate desire for outward prosperity. The apostle John desires for his beloved friend Gaius, "That in all respects you may prosper and be in good health, just as your soul prospers" (3 John 2). God certainly blesses His people with temporal prosperity. Some He will bless more than others. To whatever degree God does, it is our obligation as Christians to use our temporal blessings to the glory of God. We are to "do good, to be rich in good works, to be generous and ready to share" (1 Timothy 6:17–19).

The characteristics of the genuine believer are, specifically, a new purpose for living (not to please self) and a new focal point of concern (spiritual things first), issue in the Christian's desire to prosper spiritually. In doing so he or she is blessed. The godly person seeks first the Kingdom (kingship) of God and His righteousness. Then all by way of necessary things will be provided by God (Matthew 6:33). The psalmist in another place says, "How blessed is everyone who fears [has reverential awe for] the Lord, who walks in His ways" (Psalm 128:1). The Lord has promised that everyone who is on the path of obedience will prosper. The last section of Psalm 1 addresses the condition of the ungodly (vs. 4–6). They are likened to chaff which the wind blows away. When cereal crops were harvested, the farmers would separate the husks from the grain by a process called threshing. The threshing floor was outdoors, had a hard surface, and was usually built on a slight elevation so that the wind might more easily blow away the bits and pieces of the uneatable parts of the crop. The ungodly in their rebellion against God are useless and worthless like chaff. We saw the ungodly, namely the wicked, sinners, and scoffers and contrasted their ways with that of the godly. The ungodly are characterized as those who see nothing glorious in Jesus Christ. Nothing in or outside of them will move the natural person to love, honor, and obey the Lord with all their heart. They have no regard for His Law. They are on a continual downward path serving Satan, sin, and self. Their minds and hearts are set on the temporal and fleeting things of this world. Yes they can be religious, moral, charitable, good citizens, good neighbors, and even good parents. But as Brownlow North, a preacher mightily used by God in the great 1859 spiritual revival in Northern Ireland said of those who are strangers to grace, "They are contented without God."[13] Oh what a dangerous condition to be in. What will become of the godless person and sinner if they do not come to God in repentance (turning from sin) and exercising faith (trusting Jesus Christ alone as Savior and Lord)? Like the chaff they will be "blown away" by the fierce wind of God's righteous judgment. They will not stand in the judgment, that is, the wicked will be unable to maintain their cause. Lord! Lord! Did we not say this and do that. The Lord Jesus Christ, who is the searcher of every heart, will say on that momentous day, "I never knew you. Depart from Me you who practice lawlessness" (Matthew 7:21–23). The wicked, sinners, and scoffers all have this in common: their lifestyle is built upon a foundation of rickety wood and powder like chaff. Such a base will prove to be in the end nothing but a sad monument to instability, impermanence, and worthlessness. The ungodly will be standing to the left of Christ the Judge. They will be barred from the assembly of the righteous. That holy assembly will consist only of saved persons clothed in the perfect righteousness of Christ. They only will be found at His right hand on the day of final reckoning. The wicked will be unable to endure the trial as they will be found wanting and cast away forever into eternal woe (Matthew 25:31–46). Where will you be standing on the last day?

The Psalm concludes with the reason for the different endings of these two classes of mankind. God knows the way of the righteous. That way or manner of living consists of avoiding the counsel of the wicked, the path of sinners, and sitting in the seat of scoffers. That way is found delighting and meditating in the Law of Lord, exercising faith that never dies out, bearing the good fruits of the Spirit, and drinking the refreshing water of life from the rich deep wells of salvation. The Lord has regard for their way. He cares, approves, and directs them on their earthly pilgrimage to the heavenly country they long for. Not so the wicked. He knows their every thought, word, and deed. The all Knowing One does not approve of their way. His eye is always on them. Nothing escapes His notice. The hymn writer rightly says, "His watchful eye never sleepth." The ungodly travel along a road that is extremely wide. This road is seemingly full of life and contentment but its signposts are actually named "Without God."

They trod upon a hard, dry, sun baked road. Its soil is depleted and lifeless. At the end of this deceivingly smooth road there is a deep water hole but it is bone dry. Heaped all around are the bones of those who like themselves know not God and obey not the gospel of our Lord Jesus Christ. The wicked, sinners, and scoffers will all meet the same demise unless they part take of the healing and nourishing waters of the gospel.

We come full circle to the Biblical fact we stated at the start of this paper. Every person is in one of two conditions: the state of nature or the state of grace. We are either dead in sin or alive in Christ. If I am in the state of grace I find myself in a blessed condition. I avoid evil, delight and meditate in the word of God, and strive by the grace of God to walk as Jesus walked. If I am in the state of nature, I am in a dangerous condition indeed. But don't despair. Today is still the day of grace. The door has not been shut to the heavenly wedding feast. Today is still the day of salvation. Jesus Christ is the same able almighty Savior of sinners. Go to Him just as you are in all your sin and guilt. Admit you are a sinner. Believe Christ died for you. Call upon Him as your Savior and Lord. Jesus, who alone is the way, the truth, and the life declares, "The one who comes to Me, I will certainly not cast out" (John 6:37). If you turn from your sins and trust Jesus Christ alone as Savior and Lord, you will find rest for your soul. You will have a new and glorious view of Christ. You will have a new and meaningful purpose for living. You will have a new and satisfying focus of concern in the precious things of God. The state of grace and its abundant life will ravish your heart with love for and devotion to our great God and Savior. How truly blessed are those who take refuge in Him. Amen.

FELLOW WORKERS FOR THE TRUTH

A Layman's Look at the Third Letter of John

✠

Although the second and third letters of John are the shortest writings of the New Testament (13 and 15 verses respectively), they are "good things that come in little packages." One Bible commentator, GC Finley calls them, "notes snatched from the everyday correspondence of an apostle."[14] Sometimes we don't pay close enough attention to them simply because of their brevity. However, they contain valuable truths that address the subject of Christian faithfulness and service. These tiny gems found in the treasure chest of the Bible can best be understood in the light of John's first letter. First John provides three tests or standards which determine genuine Christianity from all that lays claim to be so. There is the doctrinal or test of truth: what does the person believe about Jesus Christ? The social or test of love: does the person love God and other Christians? The moral or test of righteousness: does the person obey the commandments of God? These three tests are interconnected, cannot be separated, and grow out of one another. Truth, love, and righteousness are the distinguishing characteristics of the genuine Christian. In his second letter, John takes his telescope and focuses in on a specific application of the doctrinal test. This Christological test concerns the incarnation of Jesus Christ. The third letter, the subject of this paper, focuses in on a specific application of the social test. The spotlight is on a real life situation seen in all its local color. We see living examples of the true and false, of good and evil, and what we are to imitate and what we are not to imitate as faithful followers of the Lord Jesus Christ.

John begins his letter by identifying himself as the elder (vs.1). We learn from the early tradition of the church that the apostle resided in Ephesus after AD 70 (the year Jerusalem fell and the temple destroyed by the Roman armies under Titus). John wrote this letter near the close of the first century. He was the last surviving member of the original apostles. He was both well known and greatly respected by the Christian churches. John had no need to call himself an apostle. He simply calls himself the elder. This can refer to an older man (which he was) but more so it pointed to his dignified person and position in the Christian community. He addresses "the beloved Gaius whom I love in truth." Although Gaius was a common name he is not to be identified with the others mentioned in the New Testament. He is a dearly loved brother and a faithful member most likely of a local congregation in Asia Minor under John's oversight.

First, observe with me that truth is an important concept in John's writings. Truth is none other than the truth of the gospel in all of its theological and practical out workings. Matthew Poole, a puritan commentator writes, "The truth is familiarly used to signify the pure doctrine of Christianity, which its principal design aims at correspondent practice."[15] The apostle Paul states that when the Thessalonians "received the word of God, which you heard from us, you accepted it not as the word of men but for what it really is, the word of God, which also performs its work in you who believe" (1 Thessalonians 2:13). When God's truth takes hold of an individual, it results in a powerful transformation not just as to how one thinks but also how one acts. By adhering to the truth of God's Word or as Paul calls it, "sound [healthy] doctrine"(Titus 2:1), this produces in its recipients a genuine love for God and others. This love in turn produces an ongoing desire to obey the commandments of God. Jesus said, "If you love Me you will keep My commandments" (John 14:15). "By this all men will know that you are My disciples, if you have love for one another" (John 13:35). John truly loves his brother Gaius. This love is a fervent love. Such love flows out of a sincere and grateful heart for who Gaius is and what he does on behalf of the cause of Christ (1 Peter 1:22).

The apostle next expresses his desire that Gaius may prosper in temporal things (vs. 2). We note that this particular desire has a distinct Christian focus. Thomas Scott observes, "He [Gaius] might be a sufferer in body or estate, or both, and the apostle desired that his life may be prolonged, his designs for usefulness prospered, and his abilities increased."[16] John is aware that his faithful brother is doing well spiritually. That he is spiritually healthy and active in his Christian walk. John is also desirous that the same be true of Gaius in the everyday affairs of life as touching his health, family, friends, business, plans, goals, and activities. All of God's people are to be useful in His kingdom. God distributes His gifts in various ways and different measures. Each one of us receives a talent or two no matter how small (even the seemingly insignificant giving of a cup of cold water, Matthew 10:42), to be used in the service of the Lord of lords and King of kings. John desires that Gaius be a faithful steward or manager of God's temporal blessings. John wants this dear brother to use these blessings wisely and properly in helping further the cause of the gospel. This Gaius did in an exemplarity manner.

Gaius's sphere of usefulness was that of hospitality (vs. 3–4). The apostle received a good report from the brothers concerning his truth which means the sincerity of Gaius's life. The Greek tense used for "testified" reveals that those who gave this report to John did so repeatedly. This was no one shot deal. No random act of goodness. This report of his walking in the truth was verified by the numerous, consistent, and faithful acts of love witnessed over and over by his fellow Christians. Who were these brothers who passed along the good news of Gaius's actions to John? They were traveling teachers and missionaries who worked spreading the good news of salvation in Jesus Christ to the lost and the building up of believers in the faith (Matthew 28:19–20; Acts 1:8; 14: 21–22). As they went from place to place with the Word of Life, be it a village, town, or city, these brothers depended on the support of the local Christians for basic provision such as food and shelter. The inns of the first century were certainly no Holiday or Comfort Inns. For one thing, most inns did not have the best of reputations. This made the duty of Christian hospitality an important practice in helping spread the gospel message. Gaius was "given to hospitality" as he welcomed the missionaries and provided for their needs. This work of selfless love became widely known to the churches. What made this even more noteworthy is that these brothers were strangers to him. Recently I heard a Christian song over the radio that had this telling line, "A traveler is far away from home. He sheds his coat and quickly sinks into the back row. The weight of their judgmental glances tells him that his chances are better out on the road."

Do you not have a comfortable feeling when you are in familiar surroundings and amongst familiar faces? When someone visits our church who we do not know or never seen before how do we react? Do we shy away? Do we ignore them? Do we put up "judgmental barriers?" Put yourself in the place of the visitor. How do you think he or she feels coming to a new place and not knowing anyone? Some churches have official greeters. There is nothing wrong with that. Yet it shouldn't be merely the job of the greeter while I await my turn to be such. As the followers of the Lord Jesus we all must make an effort to greet a visitor to help at least put them at ease. As the situation presents itself try to get to know them a little because God has sent them to us for a reason. I personally have experienced over the years the good, the bad, and the ugly when I visited a number of churches while looking for a church home. I'm not alone for several people I have met and spoken with have said the same thing. My friends this should not happen in the church of Jesus Christ whose followers should be known by a sincere love and concern for others. It is to our shame if someone leaves with a bad taste because they felt like strangers in the Lord's house and amongst His people. God give us the grace to greet, meet, and get acquainted with those who come into our assembly. That they feel not only welcomed but at ease to join in the worship and fellowship that is becoming of the people of God.

Hospitality is an important work commended and commanded in the Bible. To be hospitable means to show a friendly or generous disposition towards guests or visitors. Abraham and Lot are two prime examples as seen in Genesis 18 and 19. The Law of Moses as it pertains to strangers (Leviticus 19:33–34) and the poor (Deut. 15:7–8) is framed within a context of hospitality. The parable of the Good Samaritan provides us with a model of hospitality towards strangers. The book of Acts records many instances of hospitality shown to the missionaries. The epistles (which are the letters of instruction to the churches in every generation) exhort us to be, "practicing [literally pursuing] hospitality" (Romans 12:13). "Do not neglect to show hospitality"(Hebrews 13:2). "Be hospitable to one another without complaint"(1 Peter 4:9). We must also note that hospitality shown in its various degrees to Christ's people is hospitality shown to Christ Himself. "I was a stranger and you welcomed Me." Such works will be revealed in their true colors at the last day (see Matthew 25: 31–46).

We can be sure that hospitality is a characteristic of the faith once delivered to the saints.

John was brimming with joy because Gaius was conducting his life in an upright manner. His walk with the Lord was in line with the truth of the gospel. Think of our elders who have the great responsibility of caring for the flock of God. As they look at each one of us, are we the cause for rejoicing or do we bring heartache to them? Do they rejoice that I am walking in the truth? That I am making progress in living a consistent and faithful Christian life? That I am savory salt and a bright light in the workplace, neighborhood, school, family, and church? That I am using my gifts and talents wisely, selflessly, and lovingly in the interests of the gospel? Or do we cause them grief that such is not the case with us? As I reflected on John's joy I thought of one of the worship services at the church I attend when at my home in Pennsylvania. There was a young woman attending her last service. She was getting married the following weekend. The happy couple was moving to another location. She traveled about 30 miles to church, was involved in several areas of ministry, made a number of personal sacrifices of time, and gave of herself whole heartily without complaint to the work of the gospel. What joy I could hear in the pastor's voice and see on his grateful face as he acknowledged her labor of love before the congregation. May it be so of us that we bring joy to our overseers because we are walking in the truth of the gospel.

In calling attention to his labor of love, John exhorts Gaius to continue steadfast in the good work he was accomplishing for the cause of Christ. The apostle commends him for his faithfulness in all he does for these brothers who were unknown to him. He is exhorted to provide for them in a manner worthy of God. He is to act using God as the standard. God is caring, loving, gracious, faithful, and merciful to His people, and so should God's servants be in the way they conduct themselves towards others. Paul reminds us, "So then while we have opportunity, let us do good to all people, and especially to those who are of the household of the faith" (Galatians 6:10). God is worthy of our best efforts in helping advance His kingdom. These brothers deserved Gaius's best efforts in assisting them. They were not only fellow believers but they also took up the torch of bringing the life giving and life changing good news to those hopeless and lost in the darkness of sin. They did so for the sake of the Name. That Name is none other then that of our Blessed Lord and Savior, Jesus Christ. The apostles testify, "And there is salvation in no one else; for there is no other name under heaven that has been given among men by which we must be saved" (Acts 4:12). In carrying out their charge these brothers asked for no assistance nor accepted any from the gentiles or pagans. If they did they risked the damaging accusation of being one of the many religious charlatans out for nothing but fame and fortune. No, these missionaries like the model missionary, the apostle Paul could say, "For we never came with flattering speech, as you know, nor with a pretext for greed—God is witness. Nor did we seek glory from men [. . .]" (1 Thessalonians 2:5–6). They obeyed the exhortation of the apostle who said, "Whatever you do in word or deed, do all in the name of the Lord Jesus (Colossians 3:17). Everything they did was centered on the Person and Word of the Lord. To assure others that they had pure motives, the missionaries depended only on the help of brethren like a Gaius for support. Such actions serve as our "model of support" concerning itinerate missionaries and teachers. John continues, "So that together we may be fellow workers for [with] the truth (vs.8).

Let us ask ourselves, "Am I a fellow worker for the truth?" What am I doing to help promote the cause of Christ in this fallen sin cursed and hapless world? It will do us well to call to mind our Lord's parable of the talents (Matthew 25: 14–39). Every Christian is to be useful in the Kingdom of Christ. The servants of the Lord are called upon to work to advance the Kingdom. Everyone is given a particular talent. We are to use our gifts, time, money, knowledge, influence, position, and privileges for the glory of God. Let us not neglect the opportunities God has placed before us to help advance his Kingdom. Let us beware less we be found like the person in the parable who went and buried his talent in the ground. There are no lazy or useless Christians in God's Kingdom. Commenting on this parable, the godly evangelical bishop J.C. Ryle warns, "Let us beware of a do nothing Christianity."[17] C. H. Spurgeon, the 19th century reformed Baptist preacher said in a sermon, "He can scarcely be thought to be a Christian, except in name, who lives from week to week with no more spiritually than that which enables him to go sometimes to the house of prayer, but who, neither by his powers nor his gifts nor his time nor by any other means, ever does service to the Lord his God."[18] Let us not take such observations lightly.

How then can we be fellow workers for the truth? You may be saying, "But I don't have great talents like the one with the ten or the one with the five talents. My talent is so small. What good can I do?" Much good I say for no child of God is insignificant in the work of promoting the gospel. I like to think of Christians as a spiritual bucket brigade. In days gone by when there was no fire stations men and woman would form lines to pass buckets of water to try to put out a fire. Every person is just as important as the next along that line. Every Christian is important whether they are "bucket dippers, passers, or pourers" in the work of the gospel. Some Christians are on the front lines of Christian service. They may be a pastor (elder), deacon, Bible (Sunday) school teacher, evangelist, or missionary. They may be the church accountant or in charge of the facilities. But not everyone can be on the front lines of service due to the particular circumstances, situations, and positions they have in life. These I call the back line Christians. They are equally an integral part, a necessary link in the chain of Christian service. By the wise and faithful use of their time (God bless you nursery attendants), money, practical support, and prayers they are doing their vital part in working together with their fellow brothers and sisters for the truth.

Since the focus here in the letter is on the missionaries, what can we do to support them in a manner worthy of God? Although the three measures I will give have been suggested by Christian experts concerning a Christian approach to ecology and environmental concerns, these three actions are equally suitable to other areas of Christian service. In order to be a fellow worker for the truth as it concerns the missionaries we need to engage ourselves in informed study, planned contact, and sacrificial concern. Each of these three measures is interrelated and builds upon the other. First we have informed study. We need to make a determined effort to become acquainted with our missionaries and their work at home and abroad. In doing so I believe it's a wise investment of time to read about the life and work of missionaries from past and present generations. Become familiar with such men and woman as David Brainard (to the native American Indians), the Judson's (to Burma), Hudson Taylor (to China), Henry Martyn (to India), the Elliots (to the Aucas), Jenette Li (to China), and William Carey, the "Father of Modern Missions." These are just a drop in the bucket so to speak of the many missionaries who have dedicated their lives to bring the Word of Life to others. Their stories cannot but stir your heart and soul to action. Concerning those who labor in other places today, get to know who they are. Learn their field of expertise (a doctor, teacher, Bible translator, carpenter, or horticulturalist), where and to whom they minister, and where they need help. Churches and mission organizations have websites, newsletters, photos, names, phone numbers, email, postal addresses, and other pertinent information about their missionaries. Learn all you can about them. Let's get busy getting informed.

Next is planned contact. Based on what you have gathered from your informed study, determine to get to know the missionaries "up front and personal." You can exchange phone calls, emails, and hand written letters with a missionary. Attend a mission conference. There you can find missionaries, retired and active along with their supporters in attendance. A missionary may be speaking at a particular church in your area. Perhaps you can attend his or her speaking engagement. If a missionary is on furlough or in for a visit think about showing Christian hospitality by inviting God's servant over for dinner or cake and coffee. Perhaps you may be able to have them stay with you for a weekend. Some churches offer opportunities to go on mission trips. What better way to get a first hand look and feel for the work by being there on the very spot. Get busy making contact.

Lastly, there is sacrificial concern. I heard of a Christian who earns a living as a delivery truck driver. Each week this person sets aside a little money from each of his hard earned pay check. He saves ten vacation days. He does this to go on a yearly mission trip sponsored by his church. Not only that, he takes time out of his busy schedule to learn the native language. This way he could better help present the gospel and help counsel those who do not speak English. Not many of us may be able to do that but this is a fine example of sacrificial concern. The one thing every Christian can do is pray. Pray for missionaries in general. Then as you come to know a particular missionary, take him or her under your prayer wing. Specifically intercede for him or her and their work. A good practice every church should take up at its worship service is to pray for a different missionary each week. This will also help the congregation become more aware of those who have gone out for the sake of the Name. Not only bring them before the throne of grace but also be an encourager in your letters and emails to them. They have a difficult task.

The story is told of a young missionary who grew weary and discouraged in his work. Many who came in contact with him described him as a man with a sad countenance as he went about his daily tasks. After a few months of seemingly fruitless labor his wife took him aside. In a tender, loving, and urgent voice she reminded him that much work attended with little prayer is hard work. They knelt down together. With a full and loving heart she prayed for her husband. From that moment on the grateful young missionary went forth in a renewed strength which never failed him. Whatever you do frame it with fervent prayer. You might not be able to go on a mission trip but you can be a fellow worker for the truth by being a prayer warrior. You can also be a Barnabas, a son (or daughter) of encouragement (Acts 4:6). A year into the tragic war in Iraq my wife organized and involved the students and parents at our pre school in sending "care packages" to our troops stationed there. They put together an assortment of items such as non perishable foods, pens, writing pads, toiletries, and magazines. We received back a nice handwritten letter from the commander on behalf of his unit thanking us for our thoughtfulness and concern. The same "care package" concept can be done for our missionaries. Be a wise and cheerful giver of your material support. A song from yesteryear said, "What the world needs now is love sweet love." That is true. The world is certainly steeped in erotic love. It has seen its flashes of brotherly love. It is only by the grace of God that there is still brotherly love being practiced. I pray that all Christians will be active participants in manifesting the love of Christ to others. However, what the world desperately needs is agape love. This is John 3:16 love. It is Calvary love. This is the love of God in Jesus Christ for sinners. The missionaries have gone out for the sake of the Name to bring the gospel of true hope and lasting peace through salvation in Jesus Christ. The work is urgent. The needs of both the missionaries and the people to whom they have been sent are real. O, may God be pleased to enable us to become faithful fellow workers for the truth.

As we come to verse 9, let us note that John's writings are characterized by a number of contrasts such as truth and falsehood, light and darkness, and love and hate. We have seen in Gaius a Christian model of right conduct and useful service. The next person we meet is Diotrephes. He is not such a model. John says that he wrote a letter to the church. This Diotrephes is an apparent leader of this church. He withholds the letter from the congregation. He rejects both its concerns and the authority of the apostle who wrote it. Why? John tells us the underlying reason for his action. "Diotrephes, who loves to be first among them, does not accept what we say."

This man loved the spotlight. He wanted to be the preeminent one. Diotrephes wanted nothing to do with John nor any person associated with him. That included Gaius and the missionaries. He failed to walk in the truth. Jesus said, "But whoever wishes to be great among you shall be your servant; and whoever wishes to be first among you shall be slave of all" (Mark 10:43–44). Paul wrote, "Do nothing from selfishness or empty conceit, but with humility of mind regard one another as more important than yourself; do not merely look out for your own personal interests, but also to the interests of others" (Philippians 2:3–4). Diotrephes knew nothing of humility. Here is a person who is selfish, conceited, arrogant, and abusing his position for personal advantage. This underscores the fact that wrong doctrine or principles always leads down a path of wrongdoing. You can hear Diotrephes saying, "I'm in charge here. I'm going to do things my way." His course of action is the very opposite of the beloved brother. Gaius maintains the ties of Christian fellowship while Diotrephes cuts away those ties. He wants no joint participation. He wants no sharing of a common interest. His own agenda will suffice. This is serious. So serious that John intends to pay a personal visit (vs. 10) John will inform the congregation of this man's evil actions. Diotrephes personal ambition, fueled by selfishness, goes against the very heart of the social (love) and moral (obedience) tests John has established to determine genuine Christianity.

The apostle goes on to say that Diotrephes is "unjustly accusing us with wicked words." Not only does he reject the authority of the apostle, he seeks to further weaken that authority by means of what we call mouthing off. His wicked words are nothing but wicked gossip. As an old saying rightly puts it, "Gossiping and lying are brother and sister." Here he fails the moral test. He is in clear violation of the ninth commandment, "You shall not bear false witness against your neighbor" (Exodus 20:16). The wicked words or malicious gossip of this fellow convey the image of something "boiling over." Picture a pot of water coming to a boil. As the fire heats up and agitates the water, bubbles appear and disappear in rapid succession. This is what his wicked words were like: agitating, untrue, empty and meaningless. Yet this fellow doesn't stop with words. He carries his discontent even further by engaging in mean spirited and harmful actions. Diotrephes engages in two wrong dealings. First, he refuses to welcome the brothers. He shuns, shuts out, and closes his heart against the missionaries and anyone associated with them. He denies the servants of God basic hospitality. The Greek tense informs us that Diotrephes did this on a continual basis. There were no exceptions. Second, he hinders those who want to receive the missionaries. He acts to prevent others from providing hospitality to them. He does so by booting them out of the church. All who attempt to go against his evil dictates of not receiving and providing hospitality for the missionaries are punished. Do what I say or be excommunicated. Diotrephes fails the social test.

How tragic to toss away the Christian badge of love. How tragic his conduct. How tragic to hinder the work of the gospel.

In light of these two opposite personalities, the apostle's pastoral and fatherly exhortation hit's the target square in the heart. "Beloved, do not imitate what is evil, but what is good." In this we are reminded of Paul's admonition to "examine everything carefully, hold fast to that which is good; abstain from every form of evil" (1 Thessalonians 5:21–22). On the way to the market one day I noticed a company billboard sign with the words: Children don't need critics but models. Be a model. Oh how we need to have godly Christian role models in a world sending out so many mixed and confusing signals. Paul wrote, "Brethren, join in following my example, and observe those who walk according to the pattern you have in us." "The things you have learned and received and heard and seen in me, practice these things" (Philippians 3:17; 4:9). As a younger Christian I was greatly blessed by cultivating the friendship of my role model who was an older man. This dear brother was a great blessing in my life. I'll never forget what I learned from him by word and deed. We can also find role models in those who have gone before us. There are many biographies available of godly men and woman from whom we can gather no little profit. I recently read about the life of an early Anabaptist, Michael Sattler and the stirring times he lived in during the early stages of the Reformation in Europe. When I completed the book I bowed my head to God in prayer to make me even half the man Sattler was in his courage, witness, and faithfulness to the gospel. Your role model must be one whose words and deeds are patterned after that found in "The Role Model's Manual," the Holy Scriptures. Whoever it may be and you can have more than one role model, imitate their godly traits. Gaius is a model. Diotrehes is a critic. Be a Gaius.

John follows with the words, "The one who does good is of God; the one who does evil has not seen God." Blessed is the person who walks in the Light of God's Word. Having right views of Jesus Christ will result in obeying God's commandments. This in turn will result in a love that reveals itself by both word and deed. When we see the beauty of Jesus Christ in all He is as to His Person and work on behalf of sinners, our eyes behold His glory. We repent of our sins (which means to turn, to do an about face) and trust Christ alone as Savior and Lord. Because of our being united to Him we love, obey, and serve Him. Not so the evil doer. He sees nothing glorious in Christ. The unsaved person sees nothing worthy in Christ that will move him to love, obey, and serve Jesus Christ. Their words and deeds are evidence that they have not seen God and His glory in the face of Jesus Christ. How sad the words of Paul ring true that people are "holding to a form of godliness [religion], although they have denied its power. Avoid such men as these" (2 Timothy 3:5).

As a final example of good and someone to imitate, we are briefly introduced to one named Demetrius. This brother may be the person who carried this letter to Gaius. He also is well known and well spoken of by the churches. John says this faithful brother received a *good* testimony (vs. 12). John bolsters this evidence with the words, "[. . .] and from the truth itself." This most likely means that Demetrius's conduct is in line with the gospel. The truth of the gospel is confirmed by his life. John and his associates verify this, "and we add our testimony, and you know that our testimony is true." This brother is indeed walking in the truth and has the apostle's full support as one who is a genuine fellow worker for the truth. John concludes his brief letter by saying that he has much more to write but rather communicate it to his dear friend in person. He imparts a blessing for peace and extends greetings from the brethren. John wants Gaius to greet the brethren personally.

Third John has provided us with a snapshot of the ethical tests of life in action. We have seen a real concrete life situation at the close of the first century. Times change but human nature does not.

Since the beginning the wheat (God's people) and tares (the unsaved) have been growing together. The final separation will take place in the harvest at the end of the age when Christ returns in power and great glory. In the meanwhile let us examine where we stand in the fields of this world. Am I a healthy crop of wheat or am I an unsightly weed? Do I have the marks of the genuine Christian according to the Bible? Do I adhere to and walk in the truth? To the sound (healthy) words of our Lord Jesus Christ? (1 Timothy 6:3) Am I obeying the commandments of God in a consistent manner? Am I manifesting love to other Christians and my neighbor with an unselfish love? (John 14:21; 15:12; 1 John 3:18) Who do I imitate in life? Is it a godly Gaius or Demetrius? Or is it a rebellious Diotrephes? Am I an effective fellow worker for the truth? Am I doing my part in helping advance the cause of the gospel? I pray that our great God and Savior will be pleased to enable us to meet the tests of life. That we will shine as lights both in the church and in this sin darkened needy world to the honor and glory of His most precious name. Amen.

ENDNOTES

1   Cited at Third Way Café (www.thirdway.com), Glimpses of Jesus. Mennonite Media, Harrisonburg, VA. From *A Compend of Luther's Theology.*

2   Charles H. Spurgeon, *The Salt-Cellars, Volume II: M-Z.* (Pasadena, Texas: Pilgrim Publications, 1975), 60.

3   From *The Schleitheim Confession*, translated by John Howard Yoder, (Copyright 1973, 1977, Herald Press, Scottdale, PA 15683). Used by permission.

4   Cited at The Christian Classics Ethereal Library, Calvin College, Grand Rapids, MI (www.ccel.org/). From Matthew Henry, *Commentary on the Whole Bible. Volume VI (Acts to Revelation)*, Logos Inc., E. Stefanik, Editor.

5   Cited in William S. Plumer, *Psalms,* (Edinburgh: The Banner of Truth Trust, 1975, 1978), 8.

6   Ibid, 8.

7   A.W. Pink, *Profiting From the Word*, (Edinburgh: The Banner of Truth Trust, 1970, 1974), 82.

8   Cited at The Christian Classics Ethereal Library, Calvin College, Grand Rapids, MI (www.ccel.org/). From John Bunyan, *The Pilgrim's Progress*, Logos Inc.

9   Ibid.

10   Cited at The Christian Classics Ethereal Library, Calvin College, Grand
      Rapids, MI (www.ccel.org/). From John Calvin, *Calvin's Commentaries,
      Psalm 1–35*, The Calvin Translation Society Edition.

11   Matthew Henry and Thomas Scott, *Commentary on the Holy Bible, Volume
      2*, (Nashville: Thomas Nelson Inc., Publishers, 1979), 94.

12   Charles H. Spurgeon, *The Salt-Cellars, Volume II: M-Z*, (Pasadena, Texas:
      Pilgrim Publications, 1975), 184.

13   See Brownlow North, *The Rich Man and Lazarus*, (Edinburgh: The Banner
      of Truth Trust, 1979), 43.

14   George C. Findlay, *Fellowship in the Life Eternal*, Reprint (Grand Rapids:
      William B. Eerdmans Publishing Co., 1955), 4.

15   Matthew Poole, *Commentary on the Holy Bible, Volume 3*, (Edinburgh: The
      Banner of Truth Trust, 1963, 1969, 1975), 942.

16   Matthew Henry and Thomas Scott, *Commentary on the Holy Bible, Volume
      3*, (Nashville: Thomas Nelson Inc., Publishers, 1979), 439.

17   See J.C. Ryle, *Expository Thoughts on the Gospels, Volume One, Matthew-
      Mark*, (Grand Rapids: Baker Book House, 1977, 1979), 335–340.

18   Charles H. Spurgeon, *2200 Quotations from the Writings of Charles H.
      Spurgeon*, Tom Carter, *Compiler*, (Grand Rapids: Baker Books, 1988), 189.

Tate Publishing & *Enterprises*

Tate Publishing is commited to excellence in the publishing industry. Our staff of highly trained professionals, including editors, graphic designers, and marketing personnel, work together to produce the very finest books available. The company reflects the philosophy established by the founders, based on Psalms 68:11,

"THE LORD GAVE THE WORD AND GREAT WAS THE COMPANY OF THOSE WHO PUBLISHED IT."

If you would like further information, please call
1.888.361.9473
or visit our website
www.tatepublishing.com

Tate Publishing & *Enterprises*, LLC
127 E. Trade Center Terrace
Mustang, Oklahoma 73064 USA